HOW DID WE END UP HERE?

HOW DID WE END UP HERE?

UNPUBLISHED LETTERS
TO

The Daily Telegraph

EDITED BY KATE MOORE

Aurum

Quarto

First published in 2023 by Aurum Press,
an imprint of The Quarto Group
One Triptych Place, 185 Park Street,
London, SE1 9SH, United Kingdom

www.quarto.com/aurum

ISBN: 978-0-7112-9122-5
Ebook: 978-0-7112-9124-9

10 9 8 7 6 5 4 3 2 1

Typeset in Mrs Eaves by SX Composing DTP, Rayleigh, Essex

Printed and bound by CPI Group (UK) Ltd, Croydon, CR0 4YY

Jacket Design by Paileen Currie and Daisy Woods

CONTENTS

INTRODUCTION

"If only there was a normal, this would be the time to return to it."

In just 15 words, Neale Edwards (Chard, Somerset) encapsulates the dilemma facing many fellow *Telegraph* readers: how to make sense of a world that only seems to be getting more nonsensical? A distinct air of surreality has hung over the last 12 months: a feeling, as David Watson (Beccles, Suffolk) ably puts it, that official policy has become indistinguishable from an April Fool's joke. Frustration has combined with a mounting sense of disbelief, as the antics of government departments, prominent individuals and public institutions produced one unlikely headline after another.

The Partygate inquiry rumbled to a close, having unearthed video evidence of dodgy dancing and execrable taste in jumpers. Boris Johnson and Jacinda Ardern stepped down, while the Sussexes announced yet another "step back". Elon Musk's SpaceX rocket suffered a "rapid unscheduled disassembly" – a phrase that could usefully be deployed to cover many a kitchen mishap. Eco-activists demonstrated their green credentials by invading the Ashes and turning a snooker table orange. Everyone, from junior doctors to the DVLA, went on strike. It was suggested that things might work more smoothly if London's cabbies, never short of ideas for running the country, were given the reins of government. Or perhaps the cast of

Dragons' Den might have the opportunity? At times it has seemed that either might be preferable.

This was also the year when the culture wars spilled over into the least likely spheres of influence. Roald Dahl was held to account for his use of the word "fat", despite his having been dead for the last three decades. Elsewhere, the Bank of England weighed in on the subject of male pregnancy, while the Church of England wrestled with the question of God's preferred pronouns. Readers joined in with their own gender-neutral modes of address. One suggested "Oi you" as a sensible option, while another proffered the all-encompassing "mammals". What to do, though, about the offensive words cunningly concealed in a box of Scrabble? There are some dilemmas that may never be solved.

Naturally, there is life beyond picketing and identity politics. In this edition of *Unpublished Letters to The Daily Telegraph* you will discover readers' thoughts on everything from sex to teabags, and everyone from Thor the Arctic walrus to Gary Lineker. They have voiced their opinions on the Prime Minister's trousers and Penny Mordaunt's biceps; the fad for "rewilding" and the struggle to fit into a pair of skinny jeans; the pleasures and occasional pitfalls of getting older, getting married or getting drunk; and the best way to spend one's remaining minutes in the event of a Government "emergency alert". Often wise and invariably entertaining, their letters offer an alternative review of the year just gone, in all its variety and absurdity.

As ever, my thanks must go to Richard Green and the rest of the team at Quarto; to Rachel Welsh for casting her legal eye over everything; to Matt for the splendid cover illustration and to the Letters Editor, Orlando Bird, for keeping the desk running smoothly day-to-day.

Finally, I would like to thank the readers themselves, for their unfailing good humour and insight. No matter how we got here, and wherever we might end up, it has been a pleasure to pass the time in their company.

Kate Moore
London SW1

DOMESTIC
TRIALS AND
TRIBULATIONS

Related subjects

SIR – Why is Prince Harry complaining about being called "The Spare"? My two brothers who were respectively eleven and nine years older than me always referred to me as "The Mistake".

Stephen Peterson
Pulborough, West Sussex

SIR – In the context of what occupations will disappear due to AI, we played a game on the family WhatsApp group to come up with those offering long-term security. My suggestion of "psychic medium" was trounced by my daughter's "Parent of a teenager. There is no logic it can learn and it can never win."

Rod Buck
Tickhill, South Yorkshire

SIR – I was walking three dogs this morning rather than my usual one. I bumped into a neighbour and explained that I am dog-sitting for my daughter and looking after "The Affable Idiot" and "The Evil Genius". He replied that his wife and he were minding their grandchildren over the weekend and similar descriptions were applicable.

David Bennett
Holt, Norfolk

SIR – My grandchildren all call me Gaga. Can't remember why.

Lesley Hart
Glasgow

SIR – Why do grandparents and grandchildren get on so well?

Answer: they have a common enemy.

John Cooper
Southwold, Suffolk

SIR – My wife, who enjoyed a career as cabin-crew with British Airways, is known to the family as BAnana.

John Lavender
Port Erin, Isle of Man

SIR – Our new granddaughter is called Poppy, but I intend to call her Pops. At my age you need to get in first.

Neville Nicholson
Haverhill, Suffolk

SIR – I happily answer to Tony but I know that when I hear "Anthony" delivered slightly louder and in a deeper register I should dash for cover.

Dr A. E. Hanwell
Cheltenham, Gloucestershire

Sex education

SIR – In the mid-1960s, in my role as a member of the executive of the National Union of Students, I visited a female teacher training college. I was told that if any girl wanted to entertain a boy in her room after 7pm she must first put the bed in the corridor outside.

The Principal had no reply when I asked what she thought her students could do in a bed that they couldn't do on the floor.

Mike Thomas (NUS vice president, 1966–68)
Brill, Buckinghamshire

SIR – In 1978, soon after I had got together with my first proper girlfriend, Lynn Ellis, at school (aged 17), we were appointed Head Boy and Senior Prefect respectively.

Our public displays of affection prompted our Head of VIth Form, Mr Turner, to introduce the "Six Inch Rule", which mandated the minimum distance between his male and female students when walking together on school premises.

Mr Turner's edict met with only partial success in keeping us apart, because (a) Lynn and I sarcastically took to stalking the corridors with a plastic six-inch ruler wedged laterally between us at shoulder level, and (b) last year we celebrated 40 years of marriage.

Michael Oakey
Horsham, West Sussex

Love is on the cards

SIR – My husband has been sending me the same wedding anniversary card for almost all our married life, 48 years. It took at least 20 years for me to work out that he'd used a previous year's card as he'd forgotten our anniversary and not because, as he so lovingly stated, it couldn't be bettered.

He's had to continue sending it for the ensuing years as I haven't let on.

Judy Parsley
London W4

SIR – My niece received a lovely Valentine's Day card from her dog Theo. "Roses are red, violets are blue, I really love you, cos you pick up my poo!"

Ray Hills
Thornton-Cleveleys, Lancashire

SIR – On Valentine's Day 56 years ago I received a red rose from my husband.

This year I received a stairlift.

Wendy Strathdee
Burnham, Buckinghamshire

SIR – I have just presented my wife with a set of earbuds as a Valentine gift, at the staggering cost of £18.99.

Unfortunately the dog has already eaten one of the pair.

Roger Welby-Everard
Grantham, Lincolnshire

SIR – Did romance die when a heart-shaped wreath of oversized pigs-in-blankets was reduced in Marks & Spencer? Or did it happen when someone created a "Valentine's Love Sausage" and then had the idea accepted by the company?

Tim Barnsley
London SW16

Wedding jitters

SIR – I was sorry to read of the disruption caused by eco-activists at George Osborne's wedding.

When my best man and I opened up the reception hall before my wedding we found it was filled with smoke. My excellent best man and fellow Scouser rushed round to my mother and reassured her that although the fire brigade had been called, the "scoff" was ok.

Later my father broke down on his journey to collect my brother and arrived at the church just as my new bride and I were leaving the service.

We had given the caterers a seating plan for the wedding breakfast but it seemed that they had shuffled the name cards like a Las Vegas casino dealer.

For the party afterwards, no-one knew how to tap the beer barrel and our sound system was about as powerful as a Walkman.

These stories were a prelude to 46 years not out of a wonderful marriage.

All happiness to the bride and groom.

Will Doran
High Wycombe, Buckinghamshire

Give a little whistle

SIR – May I be exempt from Suella Braverman's new street harassment law ("Wolf whistle may earn admirers two years in jail")? A cheeky wolf whistle would certainly put a welcome spring in this pensioner's step.

Sue Beale
Maidenhead, Berkshire

SIR – Back in the 1960s and 1970s I loved the occasional wolf whistle, it made me smile and feel great! It was never ever thought of as offensive.

However, the last wolf whistle I heard was in London as I was shopping with my then 17-year-old daughter. She simply said: "Mother, that wolf whistle was for me."

Dini Thorne
Chiddingfold, Surrey

Deaf sentence

SIR – Retreating to my husband sulking room, as I sometimes do, is often preceded by an episode of HSHS, Husband Selective Hearing Syndrome, a medical condition discovered by my wife. She believes all men suffer from this affliction, and it is most prevalent when chores are to be done. Studying these two related items together might result in a PhD for someone.

Peter Bull
New Westminster, British Columbia, Canada

SIR – Who needs artificial intelligence to read a person's mind? My wife can tell what I am thinking by watching my eyebrows being raised as I speak.

Jeremy Hamilton-Miller
Twickenham, Middlesex

When you're unexpectedly expecting

SIR – Being a septuagenarian binary male, I was puzzled to receive a letter from my hospital advising a new appointment for blood tests, and congratulating me on my pregnancy. I think I will attend, as it will bring some amusement to my day.

Alan Belk
Leatherhead, Surrey

SIR – Having seen your headline – "Bank of England says that people of any gender can be pregnant" – as a woman I am thrilled that we can now give up this onerous task and pass it on to our menfolk. What joy!

Victoria Graver
Robertsbridge, East Sussex

SIR – I was asked if I was pregnant at my local hospital. "Yes", I answered, adding "thirteen months".

No eyebrows were raised and the interview continued.

Arthur W. J. G. Ord-Hume
Guildford, Surrey

Patients are a virtue

SIR – To help pass the time waiting for a hip operation, I have taken to writing, and singing along to, new words for old songs.

My current favourite begins with "I'm leaning on a lamp post on the corner of the street in case an orthopaedic surgeon comes by".

Howard Thomas
Sandown, Isle of Wight

SIR – When offered a choice of music to listen to when having an MRI scan, I chose "classical". Mozart's Requiem in D minor was played – totally beautiful and luckily premature.

Christine Cutler
Aldeburgh, Suffolk

SIR – "Protect the NHS" – that went well, didn't it?

Sarah Cuff
Ryde, Isle of Wight

SIR – No Hope Service seems more appropriate.

Alan Orton
Leamington Spa, Warwickshire

SIR – Missing: Amanda Pritchard, chief executive of NHS England. Last seen: nobody can remember. A large number of people are anxious to speak to her.

Sue Milne
Crick, Northamptonshire

SIR – Today's NHS – free at the point of non-delivery.

Nigel Dyson
Alresford, Hampshire

SIR – I assume the service for the NHS at Westminster Abbey was a requiem.

Alan Sabatini
Bournemouth, Dorset

SIR – I am now demonising those that I once lauded on the street with my saucepan and wooden spoon.

Michael Reding
Lincoln

SIR – The junior doctors have chosen a curious meme for their campaign: that of a group of small crabs.

I recall watching a David Attenborough programme whereby around 90 per cent of the juvenile crabs were eaten by predators on their way to the safety of the sea.

The British Medical Association organisers are clearly trying to impart a message to their members; I sincerely hope their patients have a better prognosis.

Anthony Cutler
Malvern, Worcestershire

Is anyone here a doctor?

SIR – My attention was caught by two items in the same news bulletin. The first was that more than 40 per cent of GPs were thinking of leaving in the next five years. The second was that, in addition to their other olfactory talents, dogs could detect the smell of stress in human beings. Is it now time for a crash programme of dog training to offset the shortage of doctors?

"Rover will see you now, sir".

David Yates
Taunton, Somerset

SIR – Some GP surgeries appear to have replaced their appointment booking systems with a series of game shows.

The first of these is "Fastest Finger First". In this game, the contestants line up next to their telephones and at a predetermined time (say 8.30 on a Friday morning) have to dial the surgery number. Those unfortunate enough to be too slow are kept in a queue for 40 minutes and then told that all appointments have gone and that they should try again next week.

Next comes "Beat the Receptionist", modelled on ITV's *The Chase*. Contestants have to demonstrate superior medical knowledge over an intimidating professional quizzer. Unsuccessful candidates are directed to an alternative service such as the local A&E Department or the NHS III service.

The final test for those fortunate enough to win in the first two games is the "Technology Challenge". This consists of a variety of tasks, such as uploading and submitting a digital image of the affected part, or participating in a Zoom call.

Only those successful in all three of these games stand a remote chance of actually seeing their GP.

Peter Harper
Lover, Wiltshire

SIR – The new GP appointments system announced by the Government is, in essence, a different way in which you won't be able to get an appointment with your GP. This will replace the old way in which you could not get to see your GP and comes after those in charge listened to our complaints that we can't get a GP appointment.

I feel we are all stuck in an episode of *Yes Minister*.

Phil Angell
Helston, Cornwall

Very good health

SIR – It has been some years since doctors were last instructed to question patients on their alcohol consumption. On that occasion, when asked by my doctor, I replied: "Probably no more than my doctor". That was the end of the discussion.

Charles Trollope
Colchester, Essex

SIR – When our GP asked my husband how much he drank during a check up, my husband replied that he drank a bottle of wine most nights, as he couldn't be bothered to try and put the cork back in. The doctor merely nodded and said: "I know what you mean, I don't know why they bother to supply lids with Pringles".

Blanaid Walker
Witney, Oxfordshire

SIR – Some years ago I had a corporate medical that included a lifestyle questionnaire.

When I went to discuss it with the doctor he congratulated me on my phenomenal sex life and asked if I achieved it because I was teetotal.

I explained I enjoyed a drink or two and he examined my questionnaire answers again.

"Oh I am sorry," he said, "I mixed up your units of alcohol with the number of times you had sex every week".

Ian Watson
Uckfield, East Sussex

SIR – Upon revealing to his diabetic nurse that for the past 40 years he drank two cocktails and a glass of wine nightly, my friend Andrew was told that he was consuming potentially 70–80 units of alcohol a week. The nurse said that 14 units a week was the recommended maximum. Andrew replied: "14 units a week? That's a dinner party!"

Rev Ian Burgess
Orpington, Kent

SIR – When asked by a doctor how much he drank, a friend of mine would reply: "I only drink socially. Very socially". There were usually no further questions.

Cameron Morice
Reading, Berkshire

Liquid lunches

SIR – I was sent, in the mid-nineties, to implement a computer system in our Munich office. I was surprised to discover a vending machine in the office selling beer.

A German colleague explained, "Here in Bavaria, beer is classified as food."

Anthony Lewis
Letchworth Garden City, Hertfordshire

SIR – A while ago, I came back from a holiday in Greece with a bottle of ouzo, to which I added my gin-soaked sloes. I wouldn't recommend the resulting liquor unless you are keen on cough medicine.

Peter Hatherell
Melksham, Wiltshire

SIR – There is an old superstition that blackberries should not be picked after Michaelmas (September 29) as the devil gets into them. On one occasion at the school where I was teaching, the children went out shortly after this date to pick blackberries for the school kitchen. The cook, being thrifty, bottled the surplus. These appeared one memorable day in winter as a lunch-time pudding. They tasted fantastic and were certainly devilish, as they had fermented. It was a very merry afternoon.

Sheila Williams
Ascot, Berkshire

SIR – Harry, my goldfish, lived for 27 years. He was revived by my mother three times with her favourite tipple, whisky.

Susan Helme
Peterstow, Herefordshire

SIR – My father's answer to the question "Do you want water in your whisky?" was always "Aye, if there's room."

Marilyn Scholfield
Whitland, Carmarthenshire

SIR – Your article on the increase in the price of wine faced a number of stories concerning the forthcoming SNP leadership election and the independence debate. This positioning brought to mind an incident in a London hotel some 40 years ago when I attempted to pay for a bottle with a Scottish £20 note. The waiter took my offering but, without moving, stared at it intently. "It's legal currency", I assured him.

"I have no doubt about that, sir," he replied. "It's just that it isn't quite enough legal currency."

Andrew Johnston
Anwoth, Kirkcudbrightshire

I'll have what they're having

SIR – Today you published yet another article on food and health. Having avoided eggs for decades only to be told that they are now considered a healthy superfood, I have completely lost faith in nutrition "experts". Instead I now look for the oldest fit person in Morrisons cafe and order what they're eating.

Will Doran
High Wycombe, Buckinghamshire

SIR – With the present price of eggs, it is no wonder we are being told to eat turnips and not cake.

Harriet Robinson
Chillerton, Isle of Wight

SIR – Are the fruit and vegetable shortages a clever ploy by the Government to help the nation achieve their five-a-day by panic buying?

Clare Bennett
Via email

SIR – Who are these people buying multiple cucumbers? How many duck pancakes can you eat?

Simon Baumgartner
East Molesey, Surrey

SIR – I've always been fond of our friends' daughter-in-law.

She rose further in my estimation when I discovered that she doesn't like salads.

> **Dr P. E. Pears**
> Coleshill, Warwickshire

SIR – When our daughter was young she would only eat chicken. She was persuaded however to eat "lamb chicken" and "pork chicken" – at least for a time.

> **Mary-Lou Kellaway**
> Cookham Dean, Berkshire

Love it or hate it

SIR – According to Heathrow security, Marmite is a liquid. Having had a pot confiscated I do hope no one in their canteen can spread it.

> **Mr J. Lee**
> Reading

SIR – When I was Administrator at Gladstone's Library, we used to make Marmite available in the dining room for the use of guests. A visiting couple from France, M. Dangé and his Glaswegian wife were staying with us on their regular drive from the Channel to Scotland. While Mme Dangé was spreading the offensive condiment liberally onto her toast, her husband turned to me, sighed and shrugged his shoulders and said: "In France, we use this to mend the roads."

Gregory P Morris
Penymynydd, Flintshire

SIR – I recently entered a competition and won a five-year supply of Marmite. One jar.

Michael Lowry
Fareham, Hampshire

SIR – My young American grandson was so obsessed with his enormous pot of Marmite that he kept it in his Eddie Stobart truck and invited his school friends to come and see it – but on no account were they allowed to touch it.

Pamela Nethersole
Hurstpierpoint, West Sussex

Crumbs!

SIR – Market research company Mintel reckons sweet biscuits are threatened with going out of fashion and even possible extinction.

I am confident that by my single-handed efforts this will never happen.

Martin Henry
Good Easter, Essex

SIR – While I am grateful for Silvana Franco's money-saving tips, am I the only reader wondering where on earth she finds "leftover chocolate"?

John Williams
Bradwell-on-Sea, Essex

SIR – One of my wife's frequent admonitions is: "You don't need a biscuit". She seems to be able to hear the lid coming off the tin wherever she is in the house.

I'm thinking of putting it on her gravestone – or should it be on mine? Either way, I wonder if it will get past the parochial church council.

Peter J. Robinson
Lichfield, Staffordshire

Read the tea leaves

SIR – In the early 1960s I was tasting fine teas in Plantation House in the City of London with the doyen of the UK tea trade, Horace Last, then in his nineties. I was then 21. I asked him about tea bags.

"Dreadful American invention," he replied. "They'll never catch on in the UK."

Duncan Rayner
Sunningdale, Berkshire

SIR – I used to use a tea bag twice then let it dry out to the point of being very slightly moist so that it could be cut open and smoked in a pipe. Times were hard in the early 1970s and tobacco was expensive after all.

Martin Brooks
Ashford, Kent

SIR – While serving as aircrew on a Royal Air Force transport squadron I witnessed an unofficial competition among the squadron loadmasters who were responsible for in-flight catering. The challenge was to see how many cups of tea could be made from one single tea bag before a complaint was received from crew members. The unofficial world record was nine.

Squadron Leader Bill Davies (retd)
Bridport, Dorset

Different smokes for different folks

SIR – Vaping equipment is disposable and, I believe, an increasing nuisance. Pondering on this menace it occurred to me that a reusable instrument, to supply the same need, could be fashioned from natural material, say wood. Its manufacture would be environmentally friendly. I think I shall call it a pipe.

Maxwell Blake
London SW3

SIR – My father could produce a sparkling display better than any Roman candle. Having given up smoking cigarettes he took to the pipe but never quite mastered the knack of packing it properly. After the ceremony of lighting the pipe, and giving a good suck, it would gurgle away before giving off a lovely crescendo of coloured sparks which would then descend onto his shirt and pepper the same with tiny little burn holes. Every shirt he had carried the same holes.

Sandra Gates
Eastbourne, East Sussex

SIR – As 1950s schoolboys my father and his pals obtained a pipe, and searched for a suitable substance with which to fill it. They decided that string would be ideal as it was both malleable and readily available.

The experiment was short-lived and my father was subsequently an ardent life-long non-smoker. I have often wondered if the events were related.

Frances Williams
Swindon, Wiltshire

SIR – As a child I used to bring back my "handwork" from school, namely basket work, to continue at home. My bedroom had an old-fashioned gas fire, so my sister and I used to cut lengths of cane, set light to them and smoke them. They tasted terrible, but we felt really cool.

Margaret van den Driessche
Merstham, Surrey

All over the shops

SIR – Some 20 years ago I bought my elderly widowed mother a mobile phone and persuaded her to use it.

She went out shopping, and I said I would ring her to test the phone.

This I duly did, and she answered by exclaiming, "Goodness, it works! But how on earth did you know I was in Tesco?"

David Brown
Lavenham, Suffolk

SIR – The most positive memory that has emerged for me during all the pandemic lockdowns and Project Fear was that supermarket trolley handles were at last sparkling clean.

Angela Walters
Princes Risborough, Buckinghamshire

SIR – I had not realised the extent of the crisis facing Waitrose until today when my wife phoned from the shop to say there was no gin available except weird (very expensive) flavoured varieties.

Michael Gale
Windlesham, Surrey

SIR – I recently bought a pack of Waitrose Essential Range pork sausages that bore the legend: "Outdoor bred & then housed in straw bedded airy barns". One can only hope that they treat the pigs as well as they do the sausages.

A. H. W. Izod
Edenbridge, Kent

SIR – My wife asked me to order a Serrano ham bone online from Morrisons, to use as a base for soup. When the delivery arrived we were amused to find that a dog chew had been selected as an appropriate substitute.

Terence Jenney
Plymouth, Devon

SIR – Due to the present economic situation, butchers are finding it difficult to produce bangers and make both ends meat.

Nic Paris
Melksham, Wiltshire

SIR – Opening a new pack of black plastic bin bags, I see that these are "fragranced", Citrus Grove, if you please. If there is a distinguished physicist among your readers, I wonder if he would kindly point out where we all entered the parallel universe, and advise us how to return to normality.

William Smith
St Helens, Lancashire

SIR – The self-checkouts at my local Co-op feature the mellifluous tones of my favourite voiceover artist and lounge DJ, Claire Anderson. I take full advantage of the otherwise remote opportunity to heartily engage with her – "Would you like a bag with that?" "You betcha, Claire!"; "Thanks for shopping at the Co-op!" "Any time, Claire, any time!"

I return to the street in a rare state of grace and fulfilment.

Raphael Channer
London WI

SIR – The Dutch have introduced supermarket "chat checkouts" in a bid to improve the health of the nation.

As I stand in the queue behind a customer and cashier having a friendly chat, my mental health begins to suffer; my physical health also, as I sense my blood pressure rising to dangerous levels.

Dr David Shoesmith
Acklington, Northumberland

Counting the cost

SIR – I always check the price per litre, kg etc. when shopping to ensure that I get the best value. Imagine my surprise when Asda was selling a 2.25 litre red wine box for £1,295.01. I know there's a cost of living crisis but I didn't think it was quite that bad yet.

Helen Willcock
Sutton Coldfield, West Midlands

SIR – For some time now, I have been purchasing packs of 100 paper serviettes from my local Poundland shop. The price has been £1. Yesterday the price had jumped to £1.50. Is this what economists call hyperinflation?

John Gibson
Witham, Essex

SIR – Shrinkflation has got so bad now that Wagon Wheels should be renamed Trolley wheels.

Sue Doughty
Reading

Buyers' recourse

SIR – I have just ordered a shirt from Marks &
Spencer. The email confirming my order warns
me that my order may be dispatched from multiple
locations and therefore could arrive in separate
deliveries. Should I also be seeking a place on a
needlework course?

Graham Lovelock
London SW18

SIR – Have any of your readers, in recent times, tried
to buy quilts and pillows that are not drab, dun, dull,
plain, pale, wan, whitish, khaki, mustard, grey or any
other insipid hue?

We, perhaps foolishly, decorated and furnished
our bedroom in restful tones, hoping to enhance the
calm by using vivid bedding. Fat chance! The only
colourful bedding available seems to be based on the
colours of Premier League football clubs or Peppa
Pig. Fortunately (purely for the moral welfare of the
country) they are only available as single-size quilts.

Paul Berry
Barnstaple, Devon

SIR – My great-uncle had been told one could buy anything in Harrods.

He went to the pet department and asked for a giraffe.

"Certainly, sir," was the reply. "What size?"

Charlotte Graves Taylor
Oxford

In hot water

SIR – Rowan Pelling's article on the relative merits of a deep soak in a bubble-filled bath versus a claustrophobic shower is absolutely true but misses one vital point. Getting into a bath and luxuriating in it is fine. Getting out of it in a safe and dignified manner is quite another story as you get older. Unfortunately a mental picture speaks a thousand words.

David Amson
Oakham, Rutland

SIR – It is impossible to scrub your feet in a shower cubicle; the risk of crashing to the slippery floor from necessary contortions is immense. As a sign in a Peking hotel shower precisely had it, "Beware of Landslip!"

Roger Croston
Chester

SIR – We always knew when my dad had had his evening bath. When he vacated the bathroom, resting on the side of the bath were his pipe, his spectacles, an empty Gin and French glass, a sharp pencil and *The Daily Telegraph*, folded to the completed crossword.

Diney Costeloe
Shipham, Somerset

SIR – Smoking in the bath doesn't work. Years ago, having watched a 1950s film with the actress modestly shrouded in bubble bath, reading a book and smoking a fag, I tried it. I lit up a smoko, picked up a book, balanced a tot of whisky on the bath edge, and climbed in. Slipped and swore, losing the cigarette in my mouth, dropped the book and knocked over my whisky tumbler – all in the bubble bath. When at first you don't succeed, give up.

Roger Fowle
Chipping Campden, Gloucestershire

SIR – The problem with using soap is that my dog steals it, and buries it in the flower beds.

Anne Hanley
Gunnislake, Cornwall

SIR – Is it my imagination that lavatory paper is getting narrower? My bathroom holder has almost an inch of spare capacity.

If this worrying state of affairs goes on, where will it end up?

Tim Sharp
Chirnside, Berwickshire

Put your house in order

SIR – I recently took three full carrier bags of books to a local charity shop. I looked forward to arranging the many books currently residing on tables to nestle beside their peers. Yet when I returned home I found that there were spaces for only a few of the waiting tomes.

I can only conclude that either books breed, which may explain those I cannot recall buying, or that libraries abhor a vacuum.

Martin Bastone
East Grinstead, West Sussex

SIR – Perhaps the Tupperware lids which disappear from the kitchen cupboard end up in the same place as small safety pins, which are also always going missing.

Stephen Woodbridge-Smith
Tavistock, Devon

SIR – Am I alone in having either fifteen bags for life in my car boot, or none at all?

Sara Dickinson
Tadworth, Surrey

SIR – My wife, an avid reader of online news, tells me that the recommendation of a kitchen design guru is that dishwashers should not be close to fridge freezers. I am now wondering how to make our breakfast without countermanding this advice.

David Beach
Minehead, Surrey

On the alert

SIR – What is the Government thinking, having its emergency alarm test sound at 3.00pm on a Sunday? Doesn't it realise that people of a certain age look forward to a Sunday afternoon nap? A whole generation could be wiped out with sudden and unexpected heart attacks.

Harriet Robinson
Chillerton, Isle of Wight

SIR – I received my alert 10 minutes after my wife. Clearly the Government has taken into account the relative importance of those who receive the alerts.

Stuart Worth
Redbourn, Hertfordshire

SIR – Is the phone alert devised to give you the chance to prepare your last gin and tonic? Perhaps miss out the ice and lemon because of lack of time.

David MacMillan
Bourne End, Buckinghamshire

Tech support

SIR – The definition of naked running informs me that I have indulged in naked walking for some time. Even if I should have my phone with me, I never remember to pocket the pair of glasses required to operate it.

Hamish Hossick
Dundee

SIR – I have just installed a new front door bell and the cordless receivers contain an amazing variety of "melodies". My wife has a traditional ding-dong downstairs while, upstairs, I enjoy dogs barking the first few bars of Eine Kleine Nachtmusik.

Dave Alsop
Gloucester

SIR – The Age of Absurdity – that others call the 21st century – often infuriates the old crab that I have become, but I must admit that my yearly tax reminder from the DVLA made me cry with laughter when it hit a record-beating level of nonsense in this wonderful notification: "If you are unable to transact online, go to www.gov.uk/vehicle-tax#other-ways-to-pay".

Many thanks to those technobureaucratic nincompoops for making my day; their complete loss of touch with the real world delightfully combines George Orwell, Franz Kafka and Mr Bean.

Yves Lombardot
Godalming, Surrey

Call of the wild

SIR – As someone who actively relishes dealing with scam callers, I can't think why anyone would pay an automated service to do it for them. I usually tell double glazing salesmen that I live in a cave. The cave has no computer or WiFi, which also deals with anyone phoning to tell me my account has been hacked.

Kate Pycock
Ipswich, Suffolk

Left out in the cold

SIR – Apparently Scarborough borough council cancelled its New Year's Eve fireworks display to avoid causing distress to "Thor", an Arctic walrus that has spent the weekend in the seaside town. My wife wonders whether the beast may, in fact, have paused in his travels purely to enjoy the celebrations. We do hope he wasn't too disappointed.

Cliff Brooker
Hastings, East Sussex

SIR – I've just heard the sound of the first lawn mower of the year (February 14). I'm not sure if this is the required proof confirming that climate change is with us now.

Paul Saunders
Thame, Oxfordshire

Growing pains

SIR – Recently my sweet pea seedlings were decimated on our covered front porch. A trail camera set up in the garden revealed 72 rabbit crossings in 24 hours, plus one cat.

My husband is taking the invasion personally and has turned into Elmer Fudd.

Roberta Hobbs
Burton le Coggles, Lincolnshire

SIR – I have had a long-held subversive ambition to submit a show garden to the Chelsea Flower Show. My garden was to be called Vita Brevis – a nod to the classical tradition which usually gets brownie points but really meant to mean that life is too short to bother with weeding and gardening. The main feature would be a lopsided table, the short leg propped up with half bricks. For seating there would be a dilapidated deckchair. The tabletop would be covered by sporting papers and empty John Smith beer bottles (we are in Yorkshire and they might have been sponsors). Everywhere else weeds would luxuriate – dandelions, nettles, brambles, docks and thistles.

Who knows – I might even have won a gold medal.

Wilma Haley
Doncaster, South Yorkshire

SIR – Following the fad, and to be in line with the Chelsea Flower Show, I have let my lawn go wild, and the bees are loving it. My only problem is that I keep losing the croquet balls.

Peter Boxall
Haddenham, Buckinghamshire

SIR – I decided to rewild part of my garden. I now have a wonderful crop of nettles, bindweed and dandelions. So much for being eco-friendly.

Richard Moulds
Louth, Lincolnshire

SIR – I dislike tending to the garden so rewilding is a lifeline.

Graeme Williams
West Malling, Kent

SIR – In the current "Wild Garden" atmosphere I am happy to have daisies on my lawn. However, I am convinced that as my hover mower approaches them they duck and when I have passed by they raise their heads and stick two petals up at me.

Dave Alsop
Gloucester

SIR – Rewilding is the horticultural equivalent of defunding the police.

Dr David Bryant
Windlesham, Surrey

SIR – While the first cuckoo of spring lifts the spirit, nothing dampens it so quickly as the first wind chimes of summer. Their discordant clanging may sound charming for all of 30 seconds, after which they are simply noise nuisance. I've considered blowing a bugle whenever there is a breeze, just to see if this would be equally agreeable to my neighbours. And unlike wind chimes, the bugle would at least remain silent when I'm not at home.

John Williams
Bradwell-on-Sea, Essex

SIR – Why is the size of trampolines indirectly proportional to the size of the back gardens where they are situated, but directly proportional to the noise emitted by the children who bounce on them?

Janet Baird
Harrogate, North Yorkshire

Puffing and blowing

SIR – Leaf blowers.

A classic and irritating example of moving the problem.

Adrian Dodge
Sherborne, Dorset

SIR – Leaf blowers are important. You blow them into a few locations and then bundle them up. Failing that, you blow them into other people's gardens and they pick them up.

Andrew Munday
Shoreham-By-Sea, West Sussex

SIR – Our golf club uses petrol-engined leaf blowers extensively during the autumn. They provide endless employment for groundskeeping staff who carefully use them to blow leaves from the greens and aprons, only for the wind to blow them back again later in the day.

Terry Lloyd
Derby

SIR – Leaf blowers are for encouraging a damp bonfire of autumn leaves to burn.

Sandy Pratt
Storrington, West Sussex

Water, water everywhere

SIR – Went for a long walk yesterday. Ditches and brooks were blocked and overflowing, roads and tracks were flooded and impassable in places.

All harbingers for a summer hosepipe ban.

John Taylor
Burntwood, Staffordshire

SIR – Have there been any reported sightings of anyone building an ark?

David Potter
Via email

SIR – I never thought I'd thank Zeus, the Greek god of rain and thunder, for being stuck under the jet stream in summer. But looking at the havoc wreaked by Hephaestus, the Greek god of fire, I am for once glad to be in Blighty.

Stan Labovitch
Windsor, Berkshire

SIR – Apparently working from home is contributing to the water shortage in our area. What are these workers doing? Moonlighting as window cleaners? Or spending all day in the shower?

Patricia Pringle
Lewes, East Sussex

SIR – There has been some discussion recently about the need and use of water meters to monitor household water consumption. In order to satisfy that requirement they would have to be rather more accessible than ours which is buried in a hole under an iron cover in the street. Since I'm not as supple or mobile as I once was, it is not monitored very often.

John Neimer
Stoborough, Dorset

SIR – I think the problem with South East Water is too many people living from home.

Mark Rayner
Eastbourne, East Sussex

The sun has got his hat on

SIR – Never mind signing up to the Government sponsored heat alert; one needs only to follow the sage advice from *The Goon Show*.
Seagoon: Gad, that sun's hot.
Eccles: Well, you shouldn't touch it.

Charles Coulson
Quarrington, Lincolnshire

SIR – It's all well and good for the nanny state
to warn me to wear a hat days in advance. As I
found yesterday, it's as I leave the house that I need
reminding.

Will Doran
High Wycombe, Buckinghamshire

SIR – Solar panels are reportedly suffering in the
current heatwave.

As my wife put it: "So now we have the wrong type
of sunshine".

Dr Simon Osborne
St Neots, Cambridgeshire

SIR – I would like to point out to the clever
meteorologists and scientists at the Met Office that
a thunderstorm warning system already exists. It
consists of a low rumble in the distance which causes
domestic pets to start looking alarmed, and allows
enough time to get the washing in.

Philip Brennan
Oxhill, Warwickshire

SIR – I wonder how many of the nannies issuing
the current plethora of weather alerts were around
in 1976. My fellow septuagenarians and I can't
understand how we have survived so long.

David Hutchinson
Nutley, East Sussex

Many happy returns

SIR – I once received a birthday card through the post, which, when opened, was blank on the inside. I recognised the handwriting on the envelope as that of my sister-in-law and so could only assume that she and my brother had been "lost for words" when they sent it. I duly reused the card by sending it back to my brother on his birthday, this time signed and with a birthday greeting written inside. As far as I know neither my brother nor his wife realised that their original card had made its way back to them, and fortunately for me they are not *Telegraph* readers and so are unlikely to see this.

Catherine Kidson
Bradfield, Berkshire

Conversation stoppers

SIR – In his article on Jacinda Ardern, Tim Stanley warns that those at a party who say they are a great listener often turn out to be anything but.

I once couldn't help overhearing in a pub a man earnestly trying to impress his new date by blathering on about himself interminably and without interruption. At long last an end was in sight when he said, "But that's enough about me," only to follow up swiftly with, "What do you think of me?"

John Bath
Clevedon, Somerset

SIR – My American husband relates a story of an old couple whose guests overstayed their welcome. The husband said: "Honey, I think we ought to go to bed, these folks might want to go home."

Pat Schlueter
Oxford

SIR – When it came to dealing with such guests, my grandfather would go upstairs and then come back down in his pyjamas and dressing gown.

Bob Clough-Parker
Chester

SIR – I had some T-shirts personalised, some years ago, with words borrowed from the Roman lyric poet Horace (65–8 BC), which read "Lusisti satis, edisti satis, atque bibisti – tempus abire tibi est!"

When guests show little sign of leaving, I disappear and return wearing one of the T-shirts. People invariably ask what it means and take it in good part when I tell them: "You've amused yourselves, you've eaten and drunk enough – it's time for you to depart!"

The investment has served me well over the years.

Robert Readman
West Bournemouth, Dorset

Sons and hairs

SIR – I had a perm once but realised my mistake when I went to the local butcher.

The lads there said that if I told them who did it they'd get them for me.

Judith Barnes
St Ives, Cambridgeshire

SIR – Is the current fad of rewilding in the garden following the trend of today's hairstyles?

Jenny Parsons
Chalfont St Peter, Buckinghamshire

Questions for the ages

SIR – My granddaughter asked if we were alive when dinosaurs lived. Well crocodiles still exist and at least she did not ask if we knew Adam and Eve.

Keith Allum
Christchurch, Dorset

SIR – My brother, ever curious on historical matters, once asked our mother: "Mummy, when you were a little girl, were you a little cave girl?"

Robin Bryer
Yeovil, Somerset

SIR – When I showed my eight-year-old granddaughter a photo of me by the Eiffel Tower, she announced I was wrong and it couldn't be me – "That lady's got brown hair".

Celia Richardson
Chandlers Ford, Hampshire

SIR – I once mentioned that I couldn't believe I had an 80-year-old mother.

She replied: "How do you think I feel having a son who's had a hip replacement?"

John H. Stephen
Bisley, Gloucestershire

SIR – My memory is getting so bad I often find I have entered something into my diary which I later cannot recognise. For some weeks, 7.30pm next Friday has contained an entry: "Peter Cook Dinner". I am an avid Peter Cook and Dudley Moore fan and spent some time trying to establish what evening of entertainment this involves but without success… until my wife reminded me that I am due to be cooking supper on Friday.

Peter Fineman
Via email

SIR – The billionaire Bryan Johnson could be partially successful in his efforts to reverse ageing and extend his lifespan through a rigorous regime of diet, acid peels, injections, laser treatment and colonoscopies. He may not live longer but it will certainly seem much longer.

Guy Griffiths
Leominster

SIR – Many of my friends say growing old is no fun. It would be so nice to self-identify with age dysphoria and change birth certificates to a happier age – for instance, 34, when one was young enough to be attractive but still worldly wise and active. Anybody who suggested we are older would be committing a hate crime despite the obvious wrinkles we display.

Mrs M. A. Burton
Cheltenham, Gloucestershire

Life in brief

SIR – One of my all-time favourite headstones simply added to the name and dates of the deceased "Civil Servant and Cyclist". I felt sure that "*Guardian* reader" was inadvertently overlooked.

Jane Moth
Stone, Staffordshire

SIR – There is a kangaroo's grave in the churchyard at Symondsbury in Dorset. It's a long story.

Liz Wheeldon
Seaton, Devon

SIR – In these miserable times I recently saw an example of unrivalled optimism.

On the wall immediately outside the Chapel of Randall's Park Crematorium in Leatherhead is a defibrillator.

Bob Ferris
Banstead, Surrey

SIR – Following my retirement I have watched more daytime television than is probably good for my health. One thing I have noticed is that a large number of the adverts are for life policies and funeral plans. One plan in particular for low-cost cremations intrigues me. It offers a 100 per cent money back guarantee: ideal for anyone who believes in reincarnation.

Philip Roberts
Caernarfon, Gwynedd

SIR – Apparently a leading mass-market funeral provider will be offering a new sustainable form of burial as an alternative to burial or cremation.

"Resomation", as the process is called, involves the body being contained in a heavy-duty pressure vessel and essentially being dissolved in boiling water and bleach.

The resulting sludge is then disposed of down the drain – and any solid residue remaining is pulverised and presented to the bereaved loved ones as the "ashes".

If the choice for my mortal remains is to go in the ground, up the chimney or down the drain, for myself I would prefer a further option – to be turned into soylent green and eaten on sandwiches. I'm not anticipating a big wake so there should be more than enough to go around.

Dr Roger Grimshaw
Manchester

You do the maths

SIR – We must get better at mathematics. Apparently 8/10 people in the UK are bad at arithmetic. By my reckoning that must be 50 per cent of the population.

Mark Lewis
Stalbridge Weston, Dorset

SIR – Rishi Sunak's plan for maths teaching just doesn't add up.

Greig Bannerman
Frant, East Sussex

SIR – I struggled with maths but received the most wonderful advice from my maths teacher, which I followed with great success – I married a chartered accountant.

Rosie Lowe
Kibworth Beauchamp, Leicestershire

School's out forever

SIR – The Education Secretary suggests that in the future homework may be marked by Artificial Intelligence. At the same time AI can also produce first-rate homework to be marked.

It seems in the future there will be no further need for an Education Secretary.

John Williams
Bradwell-on-Sea, Essex

SIR – Those that can, teach; those that can't, inspect.

Philip Corp
Salisbury, Wiltshire

SIR – Unsurprisingly I, like many in the teaching profession, have a one-word grade assessment for Ofsted.

Bethan Speakman
Blandford Forum, Dorset

SIR – My housemaster gave rather brief end of term reports. One read "unexpected talent with a hula hoop". To be followed shortly afterwards by "rather a dark horse".

Father was bemused.

Michael Wyldbore-Smith
Preston on Stour, Warwickshire

SIR – On the last day of term our French master was baffled to find his Mini missing from the school Quad. An hour later he was astonished to discover it placed, with great finesse by the First XV, in the school library. The library was on the second floor.

Dominic Weston Smith
Faringdon, Oxfordshire

Hitting all the wrong notes

SIR – The only classical music lesson I remember from school was when the teacher put on a record of The Ox Cart, composed by Mussorgsky.

When each pupil was asked to come up with one word describing the ox cart trundling along a farm track, one boy said "smelly". Class discipline was temporarily lost.

Simon McIlroy
Croydon, Surrey

SIR – Saddled with a hastily dragooned choir which was both untalented and unenthusiastic, our music teacher became increasingly frazzled as the concert at which we were lined up to sing approached. On the day before it, and in a flat panic, he drafted in a few decent singers from the orchestra, and he took me to one side to say I was the only one he could trust for the "very important" job of opening the curtain, and thus I would be unable to sing.

He later told my mother that he had "forty bad singers – but Chris was the only loud bad singer".

Chris Ash
Cunningsburgh, Shetland

Not just the birds and the bees

SIR – The sex education at my girls' school in the mid-1970s was dangerously misleading. Worryingly, none of my cohorts gave birth to frogs or rabbits.

Anne Jappie
Cheltenham, Gloucestershire

SIR – My first lesson in sex education at a Catholic school was introduced by watching an old black and white film of some rabbits frolicking around accompanied by a rather prim commentary on the difference between the two sexes. When it came to seeing the bunnies in action, the projector mysteriously broke down and we were none the wiser.

Christina Gherardi
Burgess Hill, West Sussex

SIR – A shortage of visual aids meant that my first experience of sex education involved a teacher waving an unopened condom packet to the class saying: "I'm not going to open this now as I need to use it again tomorrow."

Howard Thomas
Sandown, Isle of Wight

SIR – Lessons in masturbation and sexual technique? Oh, if only. They would have saved me years of ineffectual fumbling, many short-term relationships and at least one failed marriage.

Brian Inns
Melksham, Wiltshire

Feeling feline

SIR – Why is the girl who self-identifies as a cat attending school? Cats have far better things to do all day than sit in classrooms. There's sleeping, catching mice, more sleeping, stretching languidly and then even more sleeping. It's almost as if the poor lass isn't totally convinced of her new identity.

Charlie Flindt
Ampner, Hampshire

SIR – If a child self-identifies as a cat and is allowed to wear cat's ears, are they fed kibble for lunch?

The Countess of Macclesfield
Henley on Thames, Oxfordshire

SIR – Though I was born a cat I have long identified as a girl. A fellow kitten asked how I could do so when I am a cat. Quite rightly, in my opinion, this kitten has been called out as "despicable" and told to find another cattery. Perhaps a place can be found for me at Rye College.

Tabitha
C/o Charles Law
Hereford

SIR – Children identifying as animals is nothing new. In the early 1970s my friend was in Marks & Spencer with her five-year-old son. While in the ladies clothing department she momentarily lost sight of him and upon calling his name heard him say "I'm here" from underneath a hanging clothes rail. His loud reply to her asking him to come out immediately was: "I can't, I'm having a foal".

Wendy Farrington
Kendal, Cumbria

SIR – As a young child, I announced to my family that I was a pony. That evening I was given a bowl of grass for supper. End of pony.

Priscilla Playford
London SW3

SIR – At grammar school I had a friend who passed every playtime happily chuffing around the place – pistons, shunting and all – as a railway steam locomotive. When the lesson bell rang, he became a schoolboy again and no harm was done. That said, I'm not sure whether he converted successfully to diesel when British Rail did.

Edward Cartner
Alnwick, Northumberland

SIR – I have instructed my children to inform their teachers that they now self-identify as "intelligent".

Should the teachers then mark their work with anything less than an A grade they will be guilty of discrimination by questioning their chosen identities.

James Bisset
London SW4

SIR – I notice that Nadhim Zahawi uses the expression "let kids be kids", so clearly he has no problem should children identify as goats.

Bill Stafford
Trudoxhill, Somerset

SIR – Maybe the adult in the classroom should try self-identifying as a teacher.

Harry Robertson
Ruthin, Denbighshire

We don't need no education

SIR – While initially concerned at the impact the teachers' strikes will have on my son's secondary education, I have warmed to the cause. In support of them, I will now withhold his studies in the week prior to the usual start of the school summer holidays, and set up a mini – but mobile – picket line on a beach in Greece, in the certain knowledge that we will no longer face fines for such actions.

Don McGeorge
Bourne, Lincolnshire

SIR – At last, clarity as to why teachers need an inflation-busting pay rise, as illustrated by the picture on the front of the *Telegraph*. The individuals were all carrying that essential of an everyday balanced diet, an expensive takeaway beverage. "What do we want?" "A full-fat latte!" "When do we want it?" "Now, I finished mine."

Charles Coulson
Quarrington, Lincolnshire

SIR – I congratulate the teachers on finding two working days on which to strike in July. In my area they are only scheduled to work 13 of the 31 days in that month. I do appreciate their urgency as they won't get another chance to disrupt their pupils' education until September.

Bob Massingham
Bicester, Oxfordshire

SIR – Looking on the bright side, the proposed strike by teachers will give them less time to fill children's heads with woke nonsense.

Vincent Hearne
Chinon, Indre-et-Loire, France

Look after the pennies

SIR – What joy, the Department for Work and Pensions have just informed me that I can look forward to an increase of 25p per week from now on now that I am 80 years old.

I think I'll save up for a month and visit a pound store.

Pauline Platt
Walsall, Staffordshire

SIR – Recently I sent an 80th birthday card to a friend, and in addition to my congratulations included a few ideas as to how to spend his extra 25 pence per week/£1 per month.

– 2 or 3 baking potatoes
– 1 tin of baked beans
– 1 jar "own brand" marmalade
– 1 bottle "own brand" shower gel
– A tube of smarties
– 1 second-class stamp

Alas, only a third of *The Daily Telegraph* (which does not count).

Jean Bryant
Deepcut, Surrey

SIR – I hit 80 this week, and have decided to splurge my extra 25p on strong drink and wild women.

Gordon Casely
Crathes, Kincardineshire

Wouldn't bank on it

SIR – When the last high street bank becomes yet another coffee shop, will the working populace still be entitled to a bank holiday?

Jennie Gatheral
South Luffenham, Rutland

SIR – In the late 1990s I joined a large Swiss bank that was expanding in London. My final interview was conducted by an elegant, erudite European general manager with whom I later often exchanged ideas about his project. Over coffee one day he asked me, "Remind me Philip, what were you reading at the university?" My facetious reply was: "Eberhard, you recruited me and know perfectly well that I never went to university; I joined the Army, to kill people." "Yes, I recall now. Of course, you will find that more useful in Swiss banking."

Philip Stevens Innings
Hartley Wintney, Hampshire

The university of life

SIR – My father was always of the opinion a 2:1 was the best class of degree. It showed one had the ability to do well at university but was also bright enough to know when to stop and get on with life.

Ian Coyle-Gilchrist PhD
Foxton, Cambridgeshire

SIR – The problem of "idleness" in society is not just a feature of the present day, but was also prevalent in the 18th century when it was most definitely a lifestyle choice. A good example of this is to be found in chapter XIX of Jane Austen's *Sense and Sensibility*. In discussion with Mrs Dashwood, Edward carefully considers – and rejects – a number of career options: the church (not smart enough), the army (too smart), the law (no inclination) the navy (Edward's age). He then comes to a decision and makes the following announcement: "I was therefore entered at Oxford and have been properly idle ever since."

David S. Ainsworth
Manchester

Don't say you weren't warned

SIR – Academics have slapped a "potentially offensive" trigger warning on James Joyce's *Ulysses* because of "explicit references to sexual matters" and allusions regarding race, gender and national identity. Perhaps it would be more apt to caution readers "you may struggle to finish this story".

Ian Mason
West Byfleet, Surrey

SIR – *Ulysses* has a passage with no punctuation and Joyce is praised as a literary hero. I wrote an essay with no punctuation and got "1/10 See Me".

I welcome every effort to dissuade people from wasting their time with the most overrated author in the English language.

Robert Frazer
Salford, Lancashire_

SIR – We can at least be thankful that L. P. Hartley had the foresight to provide his own trigger warning in his novel *The Go-Between*: "The past is a foreign country; they do things differently there."

Philip J. Ashe
Leeds, West Yorkshire

SIR – If students of Aberdeen University need protecting from the traumas of a stage production of *Petrushka*, then I hope the poor sensitive souls are never exposed to a Punch and Judy show. They may be scarred for life.

Jim Doar
Consett, County Durham

SIR – This afternoon I tuned into Classic FM; to my horror they played "The Chorus of the Hebrew Slaves" without any prior warning. I came over quite faint. Can I sue for damages?

Brian Inns
Melksham, Wiltshire

SIR – Of course children should be encouraged to read but perhaps one has to be slightly careful as to what they read. My mother didn't care what books I read as long as I was reading and never monitored them. After 70 years I can still remember the look on my father's face when I, as a seven-year-old, looked up from my book and said: "Daddy, what's V.D.?"

Maggie Hughes
Gnosall, Staffordshire

Out of office hours

SIR – The recent trial of a four-day work week has shown that most of the workers who took part were less stressed and had a better balance in life.

I am happy to participate in a more in-depth, longer-term trial to investigate a no-day work week and I am sure the results will show that I am free of stress.

Always willing to make a useful work contribution – or in this case a non-contribution.

Dennis Fitzgerald
Melbourne, Australia

SIR – For several years my son worked for the Environment Agency. The blood transfusion service would visit at regular intervals and he was happy to donate his O Neg blood, not just for altruistic reasons, but to give him time out of the office with a cup of tea and a biscuit.

Mary Ross
Warrington, Cheshire

SIR – I sympathise with Tim Stanley, who resorted to covering a spotty shirt with Tippex. I was about to give a lecture when my trouser zip broke. Fortunately, there was a stapler in the office.

I was very careful.

John Stringer
Harbury, Warwickshire

SIR – Food regulator boss Professor Susan Jebb says that bringing cake to work is like passive smoking? Well crumbs, that certainly does take the biscuit.

Christine Hainsworth
Via email

SIR – As a child in the late 1970s, I remember visiting my father's office in the Ministry of Defence. He proudly invited us to come to the window, not to see the magnificent view of London, but instead to view a row of fossilised slices of cake outside on his window sill, the residue of too many office birthday celebrations. They were solid, dust covered and still perfectly formed. Even the pigeons had rejected them.

Lucy Beney
Horethorne, Somerset

SIR – My business in the 1970s involved extensive travel throughout the country, often spending periods of time away from home.

My then eight-year-old daughter wrote in her school essay that "my Mummy goes to work and stays away at night visiting her clients".

Marina Golding
Surbiton, Surrey

Reign of terriers

SIR – In your restaurant section you show a picture
of an Airedale terrier eating at a table. Last Friday my
Airedale terrier Oscar had a supper of breaded plaice
by reaching onto the kitchen surface with his very long
legs.

Unfortunately it was my supper.

Martin Henry
Good Easter, Essex

SIR – A neighbour, referring to his Schnauzer,
Angus, once told my father: "They are the most
intelligent of all dogs". The fact that Angus had just
jumped up and caught Dad in an intimate area made
this pronouncement peculiarly memorable.

Richard George
St Albans, Hertfordshire

SIR – A headline today reads: "Public urged to water
urban trees".

My two Schnauzers have been doing that for years,
as did their various predecessors.

Always happy to help.

Steven Broomfield
Eastleigh, Hampshire

SIR – I have been abroad for a while; is it now
compulsory to own a dog in Britain?

George Gavin
Broadway, Worcestershire

SIR – So it's not just me then. Dogs do officially rule the world, and certainly their owners.

Patricia Reid
Chipping Campden, Gloucestershire

SIR – Our little dog has decided to self-identify as a Rottweiler. This has much improved his status among other dogs.

Carolyn Hudson
Telscombe Cliffs, East Sussex

SIR – Some years ago, my son complained that, although nearly all dogs are microchipped for identification purposes, his elderly Labrador still insisted on sniffing the backside of every passing dog to establish its identity.

Perhaps we humans could learn a trick or two from canines about communication and not relying totally on modern technology for every interaction with fellow beings.

Christopher Wilding
Sherborne, Dorset

SIR – I am often asked, when in a restaurant, if I have any intolerances.

I always reply: dogs in restaurants.

Simon Carter
North Berwick, East Lothian

SIR – Some of your correspondents argue that dogs should not be allowed in restaurants as they can be restive, disruptive and noisy, and potentially unhygienic.

So are children – and sometimes adults.

Or so my dogs tell me. They always opt to stay in the car.

Nick Holdsworth
Newton Abbot, Devon

Creature comforts

SIR – I believe that one aim of the animal rights group Animal Rising (which recently demonstrated at the Derby) is to prohibit UK households from keeping pets, to enable the animals to live freely and naturally in the wild. All the dogs that I know and love would hide behind their sofas if they were told to go out and fend for themselves.

Elaine Mary Taylor Nomura
Harbury, Warwickshire

SIR – Our daughter's aristocratic Burmese cat lodges with us regularly and is a good hunter. Sadly she is much too posh to kill them, but proudly drops live rats and mice inside as fun playthings. She gets puzzled when they disappear.

Jacqueline Davies
Faversham, Kent

SIR – Many years ago my husband had a cat that went missing for nearly a week. On its return it came down the garden path dragging a whole cooked chicken behind it. My husband often wondered what the reaction was of the family who missed their roast dinner.

Ann Wright
Cambridge

SIR – Our son in China had two rabbits in their very small garden called Lawn and Mower.

Viv Burnie
Darlington, Co Durham

SIR – The solitary sheep on our next-door smallholding gave birth to twins.
   They were named Mint and Sauce.

Sandy Pratt
Storrington, West Sussex

The latest buzz

SIR – Please can one of the readers enlighten me why, after years of living with humans in houses, flies have not evolved the sense to realise that coming in through an open door and attempting to escape through a closed window is not going to work?

Joyce Wotherspoon
Morpeth, Northumberland

Have a little faith

SIR – I officiated at a Sunday morning Eucharist in a Cotswold church. My wife tentatively asked the church warden's wife how her husband, usually a staunch regular attender, was keeping. She replied: "He's fed up with the Church of England, he's at home putting up a shelf."

Rev Dr Nigel Scotland
Cheltenham, Gloucestershire

SIR – A curate at one of the churches in my locality was once asked why they used incense. He replied, "Well, in the afterlife you will experience one of only two smells, incense or brimstone. It is as well to get used to one of them here below."

John Dearing
Reading, Berkshire

SIR – Reading that the Archbishop of Canterbury has been fined for speeding one cannot help but think that this must be the fastest the Church of England has moved in generations.

Kim Potter
Lambourn, Berkshire

SIR – The likes of Justin Welby and their opinions are precisely why I go direct to the Gaffer to pray.

Sally Hancock
Goostrey, Cheshire

SIR – As someone who suffers from a constant spinal problem, can the Archbishop of Canterbury and the Commissioner of Police please advise me where they had theirs removed?

Wyn Rees
Bath, Somerset

SIR – I've noted the recent debate within the Church concerning God's gender. Perhaps the following may help. In the 1980s a small poster circulated the office of the contractor where I was working. It read: "When God made Man, She was only joking".

J. Meatcher
Wokingham

SIR – I find it problematic that the Archbishop of York should claim that calling God "our Father" in the Lord's Prayer is problematic.

Geoff Stubbs
Liverpool

Following the science

SIR – Now that scientists have grown brain cells in a petri dish and shown that they can play Pong, could the eggheads please install them in Westminster?

Tim Bradbury
Northwich, Cheshire

SIR – Am I alone in finding the success of a petri dish of brain cells at Pong rather disturbing? I learnt to play this computer game in my youth, but have no wish to compete with this remarkable sci-fi breakthrough.

Without any restraint, Frankenstein might be constructed before long, and I am not sure that this is a good plan. He might well play chess or do something dreadful.

John Twitchen
Leigh-on-Sea, Essex

Keeping up appearances

SIR – The shoe polish manufacturers Kiwi are to stop selling their products in the UK due to a lack of requirement for polished footwear.

Quite apart from this being a prime example of lower standards of dress in the wider population, speaking personally I could no more leave my house with unpolished boots or shoes than I would vote Labour.

Simon Crowley
Kemsing, Kent

SIR – If any of the political parties are looking for a vote winner, especially with the ladies, I suggest that a maximum age be introduced for men wearing shorts in public.

John Catchpole
Beverley, East Yorkshire

SIR – Melissa Twigg tries to tell us that no man aged over 39 should wear a leather jacket. My wife would beg to differ. After 40 years of me wearing the same leather jacket, she thinks I look great and moreover would not hesitate to tell me I looked ridiculous, if that were the case.

John Gollogly
Burton upon Trent, Staffordshire

SIR – With all the fashion discussion attached to Ascot week, the most amusing suggestion I have heard is that "fornicators" should be worn by fashion-conscious ladies.
Still giggling.

Martin Sobey
Evesham, Worcestershire

Ahead by a neck

SIR – When I joined PA Consulting Group in 1967, advice on work attire was explicit – dark suit, white shirt, unobtrusive tie, dark socks and black shoes.

Six years later, on being appointed regional director based in the Bristol office, I discovered my personnel file which included the comments on my post training course interview with the then director. After a modest comment on my potential it read: "Morgan however has a rather colourful taste in ties; he will need some guidance on this."

The colourful taste continues to this day.

Derek Morgan
Cowbridge, Vale of Glamorgan

SIR – I read with interest Charlie Brooks' piece in which he celebrated a more relaxed dress code at most horse racing events. His particular ire was directed at ties, "worn by vain men who like spending too much time standing in front of a mirror". It reminded me of P. G. Wodehouse's book *Very Good, Jeeves* in which he wrote the following:

Bertie Wooster: "What do ties matter, Jeeves, at a time like this?"

"There is no time, sir, at which ties do not matter".

Drew Jeacock
Epsom, Surrey

SIR – Once upon a time a brother-in-law asked me why I had become a priest. I explained that after leaving school – having been obliged to wear a tie for some 14 years – I swore to myself I would never have an occupation that required me to wear one.

He thought my choice of occupation a little extreme.

Rev Kenyon Homfray
Fethard, Co. Tipperary, Ireland

It's in the jeans

SIR – I was a bit put out that the article "Why it's possible to look good in jeans – at every age" only went up to one's fifties.

I'm 60 in July. Time for cords? Cavalry twill?

Mark Boden
Myddlewood, Shropshire

SIR – I can recall my first day at Sandhurst. Very shortly after arriving we were lined up for our very first inspection, in our civilian clothes. The second-in-command went along the line asking who our tailor was. I just wish that I had had the nerve to say Mr Levi Strauss.

Mike Tugby
Warminster, Wiltshire

SIR – At university in the late 1960s, shrinking Levis in the bath was standard practice, but that was only half the battle. Next you had to be dragged, in tight-fitting dry jeans, along the corridor of your hall of residence, first on your knees and then on your backside. Clad in your distressed and snug-fitting 501s you would no longer be marked out as a fresher, a group easily identified by their pristine baggy jeans.

Rosalind Grimes
Honiton, Devon

SIR – I can manage quite happily to shrink my jeans or anyone else's items of clothing without sitting in a bath of water: unfortunately for all who delegate their washing to me and my errant machine.

Lesley Thompson
Lavenham, Suffolk

SIR – I am in my seventies and I am proud to say that I have never owned, and indeed never worn, a pair of jeans in my life. This logical state of affairs is mainly down to an enduring non-requirement to chop down trees.

Ted Bourn
Waterlooville, Hampshire

SIR – I bought a pair of jeans once, some 50-odd years ago, and wore them once.

David Godsal
Winsford, Somerset

SIR – I have nothing against skinny jeans, but please do not wear them to my knee clinic.

William Tice FRCS
Southampton

A YEAR IN
POLITICS

All the presidential men

SIR – Boris Johnson, born in the US, seems to be going down rather well with some Republicans at present.

Although he recently relinquished his US citizenship I wonder whether there is a pathway back to progress through the minefields of States politics all the way to the top.

The White House needs little more than some upmarket redecoration.

Bill Wilson
Hexham, Northumberland

SIR – If I feel a ripple of republicanism, I whisper to myself President Blair or President Major. I find it goes away just like that.

Simon Longe
Beccles, Suffolk

SIR – Why is it that, whenever the issue of becoming a republic is aired, the putative president is inevitably Sir Tony Blair?

There must be other candidates. Perhaps we could emulate Ukraine and adopt the comedian Peter Kay, or follow the current US gerontocracy, for which Sir David Attenborough would surely be a shoo-in.

J. J. Hawkins
Torrington, Devon

Arise, Sir David

SIR – Would someone please put David Beckham forward for a knighthood? I fear unless he is given this prodigious award we will forever see him at every significant event trying his hardest to get one.

Tom Moore
Newcastle upon Tyne

Boris on the scrapheap

SIR – A statue of Boris Johnson made from recycled rubbish has been removed from the Eden Project. How are the mighty fallen (Samuel 1:19).

Martin Henry
Good Easter, Essex

SIR – Bet Phillip Schofield was relieved when Boris resigned. Gives him a bit of a break.

Phil Angell
Helston, Cornwall

SIR – Boris Johnson may be clued up on Shakespeare and Julius Caesar, but he should brush up on his Marvel comics. As almost everyone knows, approaching danger is detected when one's spidey senses begin to tingle. His claim to have "spider senses" that apparently "jangle" may be a sign that his survival instincts were impaired, making the outcome inevitable.

Simon Jennings
London SE12

SIR – Boris Johnson behaved rather like a pugilist, shadowboxing, ducking and diving, until he was finally caught in the corner of the ring and received a knockout punch by the Privileges Committee.

Peter Gallagher
London W3

SIR – I am no great fan of Boris Johnson, but the attitude of the Privileges Committee on Partygate has been overbearing and self-important from beginning to end.

After a lifetime trusting in democracy, I now think Guy Fawkes had the right idea.

John Jones
London SW19

SIR – We are not in debt to Boris Johnson, we are in more debt because of Boris Johnson.

Hamish Hossick
Dundee

SIR – Say what you like about Boris Johnson, but at least he got rid of London's bendy-buses.

Joseph B. Fox
Redhill, Surrey

SIR – With apologies to Thomas Babington Macaulay

Boris Alexander
By the nine gods he swore,
That the great house of Johnson
Should suffer wrong no more.

Cry shame upon those stuffy souls
Who've branded him a liar.
For truth has mattered not a lot
To Boris the high flyer.

A Tory war is looming,
Of that I'm certain sure.
But who will then the winner be?
It's hard to guess the score.

I hope it might be Rishi,
A man both good and straight
A bit like brave Horatius,
The Captain of the gate.

> **Rose Hayes**
> Dulverton, Somerset

SIR – Boris Johnson has had his Conservative Party cake. He must now eat it and stop spitting crumbs everywhere.

> **Michael Payne**
> Tonbridge, Kent

SIR – Michael Deacon says that Boris stopped Jeremy Corbyn from becoming Prime Minister.

I think Jeremy Corbyn did that all by himself.

Philip Everall
Crewe, Cheshire

Half-baked policies

SIR – With a nominally Conservative Government now considering "left of centre" price controls as a means to stem inflation, the only question facing voters at the next general election is how they would like their decline: "medium rare" under the Conservatives or "well done" under a likely Labour-led coalition.

Dr David Slawson
Nairn, Inverness-shire

SIR – Such a shame that, conservatism having won the last election, no one bothered to try it.

Sebastian Neville-Clarke
Vines Cross, East Sussex

SIR – The Tories have surely lost the next election, but we must be careful what we wish for.

I've emailed my local Labour MP to ask about the party's stance on inflation, defence, immigration and more, as they don't appear actually to have any policies on… anything.

The most decisive move I've seen them make is to announce the appointment of a diversity tsar at some point in the future. Labour is like a dog chasing a car; they wouldn't know what to do if they caught it.

Alexander Liporada
Exeter, Devon

SIR – Anyone criticising MPs should appreciate that they are a microcosm of British society.

Some years ago a relaxed and undistinguished politician remarked to me that "There were many fools in the country and they deserved representation".

John Catchpole
Beverley, East Yorkshire

SIR – I discovered an American yard poster featuring the Muppets with the slogan:

"Vote muppet, you'll get one anyway".

C. Williams
Coedpoeth, Co Wrexham

The people haven't spoken yet

SIR – Why is it that politicians always like to be seen holding a baby?

It's going to be a long time before they can vote.

Jack Marriott
Churt, Somerset

SIR – Labour's plans to extend the franchise have so far completely ignored the canine community and as a puppy owner I feel I need to write on her behalf and express our disappointment. Our puppy has already made a significant contribution to the local economy, and will be directly affected by the many laws and regulations applied to her community. Microchipped, vaccinated and put under house arrest for the first two months after her arrival in south-east London, she has a good idea of what it means to be a citizen in this country, and every right to express her opinion on how it should be run.

As long as we walk through enough muddy puddles on the way to the voting station she'll have no problem making her mark on a ballot paper. We can only hope the Labour Party unleash their imagination once in power and give all puppies their own political woof.

Camilla Kennedy Harper
London SE14

Sunak comes up short

SIR – Rishi Sunak always appears very well presented, neat, tidy and smart.

Why then do the trousers of his (probably) expensive suits finish somewhere above his ankles?

Kevin Wright
Harlow, Essex

SIR – Our current Prime Minister could be a product of AI. Pretty robotic and lacking personality. No killer but capable of a stab in the back.

Camilla Coats-Carr
Teddington, Middlesex

SIR – If Margaret Thatcher was not for turning, Rishi Sunak is a veritable spinning top.

Mark Peaker
London W1

SIR – Has the "Dishy Rishi" of his leadership campaign become "Squishy Rishi" in office?

Dr Andy Ashworth
Bo'ness, West Lothian

Money talks

SIR – I suggest anyone with a leaf blower familiarise themselves with the suction functionality in readiness should the Government resort to using leaves as currency.

Gavin Redmore
Maidstone, Kent

SIR – This Government's handling of the fallout from the mini-Budget reminded me of the cartoon character Wile E. Coyote, who, having run off a cliff edge, attempts to tiptoe back over thin air before gravity inevitably prevails.

Dominic Weston Smith
Faringdon, Oxfordshire

SIR – While I was standing in the food bank queue, my spirits were uplifted by the news that I could now increase my pension pot to £1.5 million without suffering any taxation penalty.

Chris Elphick
Slinfold, West Sussex

SIR – I note that the Chancellor plans to increase the lifetime allowance.

I hope he will also be announcing extra support for life sciences research because I'll have to work another 160 years to amass a pension fund of £1.5 million, by which point I wouldn't be much use to the economy, except as a circus curiosity.

Michael Heaton
Warminster, Wiltshire

SIR – Having controlled food price inflation by telling supermarkets not to increase their prices, for his next trick Mr Sunak will stand at the water's edge and prevent the tide from coming in.

Andrew Cranshaw
Cranbrook, Kent

SIR – Labour is saying that Rishi Sunak is incapable of understanding the cost of living crisis because he is too rich. On that premise perhaps they will only be happy therefore when the next Prime Minister is plucked from the local Job Centre.

Simon Morpuss
Stratford upon Avon, Warwickshire

Same old Tories

SIR – When I was active in local politics I was invited to a seminar at Conservative Central Office. My abiding memory of the event is not the seminar itself, but going to the coffee area during a break and seeing a then Cabinet minister puffing away on a cigarette while leaning against a "No Smoking" sign.

Has anything changed?

Peter Harrison
Harrow, Middlesex

SIR – Driving past our local Conservative Association office, I cannot help noticing that the Association Club next to it has a large sign proclaiming that it is "The Cons Club".

I cannot believe that will help when the general election comes along.

Penelope Escombe
Kettering, Northamptonshire

SIR – A Tory MP says: "We want to win." If the Tories want to win, maybe they shouldn't start from here.

Field McIntyre
London SW3

SIR – Tory MPs reacting like infantile Tik Tok Twitterers should join the Red Wall, socialist, high tax, low productivity Labour and Liberal parties – because that's what they are endorsing.

Bill Todd
Whitton, Middlesex

SIR – I do hope the new chairman of the Conservative Party is indeed a conservative, although I do appreciate this would put them at odds with the majority of their Cabinet colleagues.

Paul Vince
Trowbridge, Wiltshire

SIR – Aren't we overdue a Tory leadership challenge and race?

It seems weeks since the last one.

Michael West
Poole, Dorset

SIR – Supporting the Conservative Party is like supporting a perpetually losing football team – losing because a third of the players systematically and deliberately score own goals.

Henry Speer
Lincoln

SIR – This week I have been teaching sailing to an American woman in her thirties.

She said "I don't know much about English politics – I didn't know that the Conservatives were the Tories". I replied: "I don't think at the moment the Conservatives know themselves that they are the Tories."

T. W. Wood
Colchester, Essex

SIR – If the Conservative Government were a dog, it would have been taken to the vet and put to sleep some time ago.

W. K. Wood
Bolton, Lancashire

Things can only get worse?

SIR – I agree with Prince Harry that the Government has reached rock bottom.

But I fear that they have now started drilling.

Peter Hopper
Stevenage, Hertfordshire

SIR – With so many changes at No 10 and No 11 Downing Street, should I buy shares in Pickfords?

Roger Foord
Chorleywood, Hertfordshire

SIR – Will stab vests be provided to any new member of government?

Rob Dorrell
Bath, Somerset

SIR – "Wallace rules out move to top Nato job", says your headline. Have they asked Gromit?

Geoffrey Nobes
Locks Heath, Hampshire

Credit Suisse in meltdown

SIR – It seems a strange coincidence that Credit Suisse has gone into liquidation at the same time as its glaciers.

Fiona Wild
Cheltenham, Gloucestershire

SIR – How did Credit Suisse become Debit Suisse so quickly without anyone knowing?

Andrew Harding
Haywards Heath, West Sussex

Ask the experts

SIR – Is there any chance we can have the cast of *Dragons' Den* drafted in to run the country? Or perhaps Martin Lewis?

Deidre Burton
Newmarket, Suffolk

SIR – Most taxi drivers are free with their political observations and clearly have better ideas for running the country than our present statesmen. Could we not affect a swap in professions?

Come to think of it, the present bunch in the Commons would be pretty useless at general knowledge, let alone "the Knowledge".

Arthur W. J. G. Ord-Hume
Guildford, Surrey

Vote of no confidence

SIR – I recently went to lunch with a friend of mine and we got into a political debate. He asked me who I was going to vote for at the next general election. I told him that I would probably vote for Reform UK because I couldn't possibly vote for any left-wing party. He said, "Surely the Conservatives are standing in your constituency as well". I replied, "Yes they are, but as I just said, I couldn't possibly vote for any left-wing party".

Mike Adams
Defford, Worcestershire

SIR – I will not be voting at the next general election. However, as a woman, I will use my vote; not to do so would be disrespectful to all those who fought for my right to vote.

I have decided, therefore, to write "Foxtrot Oscar" across the ballot paper.

Yvonne A. Frith
Sidmouth, Devon

SIR – The impending general election would be a perfect opportunity to hold a plebiscite on matters of public importance. The incoming government would then know whether the vast majority of people really are in favour of Just Stop Oil (et al), background music, Channel migration, Gary Lineker, The BBC licence, Net Zero, and HS2, just to name but a few.

Keith Macpherson
Clevedon, Somerset

SIR – When I see people voting for the Green Party I long for the good old days when the Monster Raving Loony party offered a solid and plausible alternative to Labour or the Conservatives.

The Green Party live in la la land and they should stay there.

Mick Ferrie
Mawnan Smith, Cornwall

SIR – When describing the UK political landscape to one of the grandchildren I explained it by stating that a Jaguar is the best indicator.

Seeing a shiny new Jaguar, the Labour Party says, "What can we do to remove that from its owner?" The Conservative says, "What do I need to do to own one like that? The liberals say, "That car is a symbol of oppression and the owner must be publicly chastised for daring to work hard and save."

But the Remainers and the EU civil servants say, "Due to my position and regular attendance in committee meetings I should be given a chauffeur-driven one to demonstrate my importance."

We who want to own a Jag are prepared to work for one and don't see it – or the award of honours – as a natural perk of work.

David Hyman
Manchester

Sir Keir called into question

SIR – Ten times Nick Ferrari (LBC Radio) asked the same question; ten times Sir Keir Starmer was evasive and failed to provide an answer.

Perhaps he is prime ministerial material after all.

Jonathan Mann
Gunnislake, Cornwall

SIR – You reported that the Labour leader had taken a stand on an issue.

Perhaps the fence has collapsed.

James Sharp
Wareham, Dorset

SIR – With the arrival of warmer weather I am conscious of the need to refresh my summer wardrobe and specifically purchase a new pair of Starmers – previously known as flip flops.

Richard Holdron
Wisbech, Cambridgeshire

SIR – Should Keir Starmer's continued ability to firmly believe in opposing positions now qualify him to replace Schrödinger's cat?

Paul Saunders
Thame, Oxfordshire

Servants of the people

SIR – Dickens's novels were set in the 19th century and many features like the Marshalsea debtors' prison have long since disappeared.

However, when one reads of the sclerosis of the State's workings, it is evident that the Circumlocution Office still pertains and the Tite Barnacles are, indeed, flourishing.

John Taylor
Hammerwich, Burntwood

SIR – When scanning ahead in your Review pages to look for interesting TV programmes, I came across one which I thought might be a documentary about the Civil Service.

It was described as "The Blob: a Genius without a Brain. An organism that challenges the concept of intelligent life."

C. A. Anderson
Ravensheugh, Selkirkshire

SIR – Critics of the appointment of Sue Gray as Sir Keir Starmer's chief of staff argue that it undermines the impartiality of the Civil Service. That ship hasn't merely sailed. It has long since sunk.

David Miller
Chigwell, Essex

SIR – The British army introduced a new infantry rifle in the 1980s. As a result of its unreliability, squaddies quickly named it "The civil servant" – "doesn't work, can't fire it".

Gerard Somers
Atherstone, Warwickshire

SIR – My son, who ran the London Marathon, reports that it was brilliantly organised. Clearly the Civil Service was not involved.

Peter Munro
Wincanton, Somerset

SIR – After an interview for the economics fast stream in 2003 I was told that I am entirely unsuitable to be a civil servant.

I now take that as a compliment.

Oliver Ranson
Newcastle upon Tyne

SIR – Dave Penman, the senior civil servants' union boss, says it's unfair to call Whitehall mandarins "lazy, woke, inefficient, Remainer, activist snowflakes" who use "Machiavellian" methods to frustrate Conservative policy and unseat ministers.

He is quite right regarding "lazy" because they work tirelessly at all the rest.

Martin Burgess
Beckenham, Kent

Sending the wrong message

SIR – I had just finished reading today's reports on the Lockdown Files, when I received a text from my GP surgery telling me I needed to have a blood pressure check.

How did they know?

Anthony Tanney
Wickham Bishops, Essex

SIR – To the 2.3 million words you are currently sifting through, may I add a few of my own?

Disingenuous, self-serving, incompetent, egomaniacal and backstabbing should probably be enough for starters.

Mike Tugby
Warminster, Wiltshire

SIR – Please would you print a trigger warning on the front page of *The Daily Telegraph* whenever there are photos of Matt Hancock included anywhere in the newspaper?

Perry Bebbington
Kimberley, Nottinghamshire

SIR – I've been struggling to determine what I should give up for Lent this year. You have provided an easy answer. I am banning myself from reading anything about Matt Hancock.

Alan Frost
Bournemouth, Dorset

SIR – Matt Hancock: wrong man, wrong time, wrong place.

Tim Baker
Petersfield, Hampshire

SIR – Scheming politicians? Goodness gracious. Whatever next?

Nairn Lawson
Portbury, Somerset

An uncivil war

SIR – Reading the ongoing coverage of Dominic Raab's resignation I have come to realise how much I have been bullied for the past 15 years by my cat, Fred.

The constant demands for food, the destruction of household items, the 6am calls and the regular delivery of dead rodents, which terrorise the household, have taken their toll. One must also take account of the rising vets' bills and the jealousy of realising that he is never on a waiting list for treatment. However, I chose to have him, in much the same way as people decide to have a career in the Civil Service.

Mark Robbins
Bruton, Somerset

SIR – It is my considered opinion that Mr Sunak should have thanked Mr Raab for his letter of resignation – and then told him to go back to work.

Brian Gedalla
London N3

SIR – One assumes poor Dominic just raabs people up the wrong way.

Mark Peaker
London W1

SIR – I understand that Labour is calling for an urgent inquiry into the allegation that Suella Braverman left a toilet seat in the upright position in 2022.

Roger Burrows
Bishops Stortford, Hertfordshire

SIR – We left the EU to get away from unelected bureaucrats governing us but now we have the Prime Minister asking an unelected bureaucrat to decide on sacking a minister.

I suppose it is at least a British unelected bureaucrat.

Keith Murdoch
Stansted, Kent

Now that the party's over

SIR – I have been of the opinion that HS2 was the greatest waste of money yet devised, but watching the proceedings of the Partygate inquiry I may have to change my opinion.

Richard Loates
London SW14

SIR – Is it not time there was a full and exhaustive public inquiry into the number of public inquiries?

Neil Stuart
Tavistock, Devon

SIR – The House of Commons Committee of Privileges has published its report into their view of Mr Johnson's veracity. It does not seem to have received universal acclaim but I do hear that some Australian marsupials are delighted with it.

Ian Goddard
Wickham, Hampshire

SIR – To label the report of the House of Commons Committee of Privileges on the conduct of Boris Johnson as the output of a kangaroo court is frankly insulting to kangaroos, who are fine upstanding animals.

David Bell
Knowl Hill, Berkshire

SIR – You should never lose your sense of humour with British politics. When you have Chris "Underpants" Bryant and Alastair "Iraq War" Campbell putting themselves forward as arbiters of probity and decency you know you are reaching peak comedy.

Simon Roxborough
St Helens, Lancashire

SIR – A suggestion aired on BBC Radio 4 was that the stacks of redundant plastic PPE, ineptly procured during the pandemic, might be incinerated to generate energy.

Perhaps, next time, our government might cut out the middle man, and simply incinerate £20 notes.

Graham Clifton
Kingston upon Thames, Surrey

SIR – Gatherings or parties? Perhaps it is a matter of degree. At a work gathering you do not get drunk and chase the interns around the photocopier, whereas at a party…

Ian McMullen
Smarden, Kent

SIR – The video showing Conservative Party staff partying during lockdown was truly shocking – the dancing was terrible.

Captain Graham Sullivan RN (retd)
Gislingham, Suffolk

SIR – Why doesn't the Government ask ChatGPT to write the report into Partygate? Then the major expense would be the felt tip required to redact the names.

John Parsons
Ross-on-Wye, Herefordshire

They protest too much

SIR – If Extinction Rebellion and Animal Uprising et al would like to inform me when they have wedding anniversaries, weddings, christenings and birthdays, I'd be very happy to disrupt them.

It seems only fair.

Patrick Fuller
Upper Farringdon, Hampshire

SIR – I would very much like to know the brand of glue being used by Just Stop Oil activists.

It really does seem to stick anything to anything.

Andrew Bourn
Harrogate, North Yorkshire

SIR – Didn't the Just Stop Oil protesters notice that a snooker table is just about as green as it gets?

Stuart D. Oakley
Leiden, The Netherlands

SIR – Regardless of one's opinions about their cause, it is worth acknowledging the remarkable efficacy of the Just Stop Oil protesters in securing tickets for everything.

David McCreadie
South Harting, West Sussex

SIR – Perhaps the environmental protesters would have more impact if they were to spend their time studying sciences and engineering and then coming up with viable alternatives to oil.

John Gander
Worthing, West Sussex

SIR – Activists want Britain to restitute artefacts taken during the period of the British Empire.

I would like to apologise for – and return – the Danegeld, but it's all gone.

Andrew Dane
Pocklington, East Yorkshire

Natural gas

SIR – You report that cows can be given food which reduces their flatulence. Is there something similar available for humans? It would improve everyone else's quality of life.

Helen Bones
Farnham Common, Buckinghamshire

SIR – If an overseer is appointed to take charge of the attempt to reduce bovine-produced methane, at least the person will have the only appropriate title for this sort of sinecure: Hot Air Tsar.

Anne Jappie
Cheltenham, Gloucestershire

SIR – The perfect way to obtain global "net zero" carbon emissions would be to exterminate the entire human race.

R. L. Smith
Bristol

Running low on energy

SIR – It appears that the Labour Party has replaced the Magic Money Tree with a new Magic Energy Tree, one that produces constant power from nowhere.

R. Fleming
Leicester

SIR – Reading Labour's plans and proposals for an energy policy I am made mindful of the need to stock up on board games and candles.

Charles Penfold
Ulverston, Cumbria

SIR – Wind power and socialism are fine in theory but unfortunately they don't work in practice.

J. A. Rolph
Towcester, Northamptonshire

SIR – Britain has had a large wind farm for many years now. It is called the Palace of Westminster.

Michael Bristow
Bristol

SIR – We have a government department called The Department for Energy Security and Net Zero.
   Surely the "and" should be an "or".

Philip Franklin
Wellesbourne, Warwickshire

SIR – We may be paid £10 a day to get us to put the washing machine on at night.
   Barmy! What's wrong with asking us nicely?

Susan Bye
Arnold, Nottinghamshire

SIR – One of the great joys in life is hanging washing outside, preferably with a suitable wind blowing. This drying process comes free.

If washing is to be done during the night to save energy, as the Government recommends, not only will a pleasurable task not be possible but by morning, the clothes will be creased thus requiring more effort to iron. Also, greater expense will be incurred in usage of dryers. Relationships with sleeping neighbours might not improve either.

Margaret Wood
Aberdeen

The eyes of the law

SIR – Thames Valley Police have advised me that a police officer will be in Ascot High Street on Sunday January 29. Such a rare appearance will doubtless bring out the crowds in their thousands.

Duncan Rayner
Sunningdale, Berkshire

SIR – If I lie down wearing a high-vis jacket at the entrance road to the Houses of Parliament, will the police do anything? I want to protest at the police not doing their job.

Christopher Hunt
Swanley, Kent

SIR – A helpful London copper once explained the rules of busking to me. If I was rubbish I would be moved on for causing a disturbance; if I was good and attracted a crowd I would be moved on for obstructing the highway, but if I was bland and inoffensive I would be left alone.

Julian S. Badenoch
Cowes, Isle of Wight

SIR – If you require a policeman for a crime or anything else, first glue yourself to a nearby anything – preferably with a placard saying cats are dangerous or any other tripe – and, bingo, a team of police will arrive. While they are ministering to your every need, casually mention the burglar you have attacked inside your property.

Howard Boothroyd
Kirkburton, West Yorkshire

Welcome to Scotland

SIR – In the event that Scotland gains independence, led by Nicola Sturgeon, will millions of Scottish people flock back to the country or will millions leave?

Simon McIlroy
Croydon, Surrey

SIR – In highlighting the parlous life expectancy figures in Scotland, Alan Cochrane's article reminded me that it was Alex Salmond who called the independence referendum a "once in a generation opportunity".

Nicola Sturgeon described it as "once in a lifetime".

A cynic could be forgiven for thinking she may have been on to something.

Guy Bargery
Edinburgh

SIR – Keith Brown, deputy leader of the SNP, is quite correct when he says the SNP is the most transparent party in Scotland.

Everybody can see through them.

Tony Cowan
Elgin, Moray

SIR – Given Kate Forbes' willingness to stand up for historic Christian teaching and Justin Welby's refusal to do the same, perhaps we could arrange a transfer so that she becomes leader of the Church of England and he joins the SNP.

Andrew Berkinshaw-Smith
Walton-on-Thames, Surrey

The measure of a woman

SIR – Surely the debate as to whether the convicted rapist Isla Bryson/Adam Graham is a man or a woman is focusing on the wrong question.

By studying the wig, the clothes and the makeup, we are surely re-enforcing the very same stereotypes that we were all told were patriarchal.

Perhaps Nicola Sturgeon's legislation can specify more pertinent questions, such as whether this person can multi-task, can listen attentively, can follow simple instructions and, when opening the fridge, can see what is right there.

Rowland Aarons
London N3

Sturgeon wants her independence

SIR – Will Nicola Sturgeon hold a second resignation if this one does not work?

Jonny Gray
Edinburgh

SIR – How magnanimous of Nicola Sturgeon to apologise for historic events for which she was not responsible. She seems strangely silent on things for which she was responsible.

Ian Maddock
Alveley, Shropshire

SIR – Nicola Sturgeon's end-of-term school report would indicate that she did very well with her work but could have tried harder in the end to make her political performance more arresting.

Dennis Forbes Grattan
Aberdeen

SIR – Nicola Sturgeon, whatever one's opinion, cannot be accused of lacking an even-handed approach in her dealings with the UK Government.

This usually involved holding a begging bowl in one hand, and making a clenched fist with the other.

C. J. Rawson
Burnley, Lancashire

SIR – After watching and listening to the farcical cobbled-together policies of the candidates for the First Minister's position I cannot get the Judy Collins song *Send in the Clowns* out of my head.

Allan Thompson
Glasgow

Britain isn't working

SIR – I hear that the DVLA has commenced a five-day strike. Will anyone notice?

Rob Mason
Sandhurst, Berkshire

SIR – I assume that the 100,000 civil servants who are going to strike will be picketing their own front doors.

Phil Coutie
Exeter, Devon

SIR – Other than providing a convenient scapegoat for missing Christmas cards that I actually forgot to send, have the strikes by postal workers achieved anything?

Martyn Pitt
Gloucester

SIR – It seems that the "welfare" safety net has morphed into a hammock.

Dot Marshall-Gent
Whitstable, Kent

SIR – This is getting serious. Strike action by nurses, doctors, rail staff, Tube staff, binmen and, er, actors. It'll be the poets next and then where will we be?

John Ryall
Crowborough, East Sussex

SIR – As an old pensioner struggling to make ends meet I was considering going on strike like the rest of the country. However, the allotment getting overgrown would only add to my problems.

Nairn Lawson
Portbury, Somerset

Don't break the bank

SIR – (to the tune of Gilbert and Sullivan)

Andrew Bailey is the very model of a modern Governor General,
blaming his vicissitudes on information vegetable, animal and
mineral.

Claiming to know what is meant by inflationary but making it
incendiary.

Simon Warde
Bognor Regis, West Sussex

SIR – Inflation is like toothpaste. Once it is out of the tube it is extremely difficult to get it back in again.

John Savage
Bovey Tracey, Devon

SIR – I have noticed that since bank managers stopped wearing ties a lot of banks have failed.

I hope that Jeremy Hunt, the Chancellor of the Exchequer, continues to wear his tie.

Clive Hilton
Bradford-on-Avon, Wiltshire

SIR – It was a great relief to read that our inflation is due to Brexit and not the Bank of England's prolonged quantitative easing and extraordinary low interest rates.

Derek G. Machin
Caldy, Wirral

SIR – As so many financial institutions seem to be debarring clients because of views of which the former disapprove, I hope that HMRC joins in the fray when I express a "disapproved" view.

Michael Turner
Winchester, Hampshire

SIR – Many banks were saved by British taxpayers a few years ago. I wonder if those banks paused to worry that some of their huge bailouts came from taxpayers with politically incorrect views?

John G. Smith
London N11

SIR – There is much I have to say on the treatment of Nigel Farage by Coutts, but I am now terrified to express my views in case the bank reads my letter.

Janet Warwick
Shipton under Wychwood, Oxfordshire

SIR – Coutts's Reputational Risk Committee has done more harm to their reputation than any of their clients could have achieved.

Nik Perfitt
Bristol

SIR – In order to demonstrate its commitment to diversity and inclusivity Coutts Bank needs its quota of angry old white men. I offer my services, for a fee.

James Masters
Bucknell, Shropshire

SIR – Thank goodness that the NatWest boss Dame Alison Rose has fallen on her cheque book.

Malcolm Watson
Ryde, Isle of Wight

Leave to Remain

SIR – I'm very happy to have another vote on Brexit. There was a gap of over 40 years before the 2016 vote so around 2056 sounds good to me.

John Frankel
Newbury, Berkshire

SIR – I watched the tide come in today. And then it did a complete U-turn and went out again. It would not have done that before Brexit.

Patrick Smith
Great Yarmouth, Norfolk

SIR – Brexit bashing appears to be the fashionable field sport these days for the most illogical of reasons. Of course what cannot be denied is the performance and unprecedented success of our tennis players at the start of the grass court season this year against strong European opposition. It can only be attributed to the benefits of Brexit. At this rate Andy Murray will win Wimbledon again.

Chris Hunt
Swanley, Kent

SIR – Daniel Hannan suggests that Brexit was like moving house and worries about the UK rejoining the EU by stealth. Having moved from a comfortable home in the suburbs we now appear to be living in a dilapidated shack on the edge of town. His anxiety is well founded.

Dean Johnson
East Rudham, Norfolk

SIR – Should there be a need to modify the Windsor framework because of DUP pressure, I assume it will become a Half Windsor. If it fails completely, a Full Windsor Knot.

Nigel Algar
Bottesford, Nottinghamshire

Who's in and who's out

SIR – There is now clear water between Labour and the Conservatives on immigration. Labour won't make any attempt to control it while the Conservatives will promise to but fail.

John Stewart
Terrick, Buckinghamshire

SIR – The immigration minister Robert Jenrick says that the Government is not complacent over immigration. It must be incompetence then.

David Miller
Chigwell, Essex

SIR – Rather than paint over the mural of Mickey Mouse at the Kent reception centre for unaccompanied child asylum seekers, it should be moved to the Home Office foyer for display as a fitting symbol of what goes on there.

Edward Hill
Chandlers Ford, Hampshire

SIR – In view of the obvious lack of control of our borders, perhaps we should enlist the help of Captain Mainwaring and his platoon to patrol the beaches.

Lovat Timbrell
Brighton, East Sussex

Go with the territory

SIR – Sick of being mistreated and ignored by Westminster and Edinburgh? Orkney residents are, so their council is considering applying to become a territory of Norway. What a splendid idea! Could we please have a similar vote here in the ancient Viking territory of East Anglia?

Angela Lawrence
Woodbridge, Suffolk

SIR – How I envy the right and ability of the islanders of Orkney to secede from Westminster and Holyrood. The UK is a madhouse, and the rest of us are stuck with it.

Neil Poucher
Caistor, Lincolnshire

Rise of the machines

SIR – Out of idle curiosity I asked the AI chatbot ChatGPT whether it was out to conquer the world. The response was that it did not understand my question. So it seems it might be more human than I could have possibly imagined.

Alan Dyer-Perry
Poundbury, Dorset

SIR – Singer-songwriter Sting says that musicians will face a "battle" as they are forced to compete with the rise of AI.

But is he worrying unnecessarily?

After all, how could AI emulate lyrics like "De Do Do Do, De Da Da Da"?

Geoff Johnson
Gateshead, Co Durham

SIR – The computer scientist Dr Geoffrey Hinton is right to fear that robots could become smarter than humans. It is not a high bar.

Derek Wellman
Lincoln

SIR – I think we should be more welcoming to AI considering how well NS (natural stupidity) appears to be running things at the moment.

Julian S. Badenoch
Cowes, Isle of Wight

SIR – I note the problems expressed about robots and their damaging potential. I suggest that the problem be referred to Dr Who. He it was who succeeded in outsmarting the scientist Hilda Winters and the robot she had designed to destroy those with whom she disagreed. Miss Winters was sentenced to 20 years' imprisonment for her pains. I write as the actress who portrayed her, still chastened from her experience at the hands of the good Doctor.

Patricia Maynard
Alton, Hampshire

SIR – The new minister for science, Michelle Donelan, has suggested that AI should be seen as "an opportunity". The civil service is looking into AI to write Government policy. I'm reminded of Eric Idle's "Galaxy Song" in which the last verse is:
So remember
when you're feeling very small and insecure
How amazingly unlikely is your birth
And pray that there's intelligent life
somewhere up in space
'Cause there's b----- all down here on Earth.
We'll soon be compelled to apply Isaac Asimov's three laws of robotics.

Still, also in the same newspaper, microbial life may have been found on Mars. There's still hope.

Peter Wickison
Driffield, East Yorkshire

SIR – Why should we treat AI as if it were a new threat? We already have killer robots. They are in place as the leaders of Russia, North Korea and Iran.

Robin Motts-Gardiner
Melksham, Wiltshire

It's a funny old world

SIR – With the current state of affairs it's not surprising to learn that more people are turning to laughing gas. It's that or cry.

Mark Wade
Reading, Berkshire

SIR – It is now impossible to tell the difference between government policy and an April Fool's Day joke.

David Watson
Beccles, Suffolk

SIR – At the behest of my wife, we recently conducted a purge of our bookshelves. Among the pile was a 2009 book by Quentin Letts, entitled *50 People Who Buggered up Britain*. Time for an updated version?

Mike Ostick
Upton upon Severn, Worcestershire

SIR – If only there was a normal, this would be the time to return to it.

Neale Edwards
Chard, Somerset

THOUGHTS ON ABROAD

Slow to arms

SIR – The German ambassador, being interviewed on the BBC about Germany's procrastination regarding tanks for Ukraine, stated: "We are worried about our future relations with Russia".

Surely a candidate for quote of the year and January is not yet over.

Illtyd Lewis
London SW6

SIR – It is a pity that the Germans are slow with their tanks yet so fast with their towels.

John Hickman
Wantage, Oxfordshire

Another time, another war

SIR – Our fathers, grandfathers and great-grandfathers fought in two world wars to rid this planet of thugs like Putin. Nearly 80 years later, where are we? No further forward than we were in 1945.

E. W. Parkman
Eastbourne, East Sussex

SIR – Last night, our Ambassador in Moscow handed Vladimir Putin a final note, stating that, unless we heard from him by noon today that he was prepared, at once, to withdraw his forces from Ukraine, we would be forced to misgender him.

I have to tell you now that no such undertaking has been received, and that, consequently, Vladimir Putin is a girly swot.

That should show him.

Adam Massingham
Ashford, Kent

SIR – In his incompetent war against a highly motivated Ukrainian army Vladimir Putin is about to discover the truth in the old adage "one volunteer is worth ten pressed men".

Jonathan Carr
Shrewsbury, Shropshire

SIR – President Putin poses a far greater immediate threat to life on our planet than any asteroid. It's a pity that Nasa's DART defence technology cannot be put to good use closer to home.

Eleanor Peal
Yelling, Cambridgeshire

SIR – Given the nuclear threat currently posed by Russia, I can't help but wonder if misguided eco activists might be far more effective in saving the planet by gluing Vladimir Putin to the road rather than themselves.

Martyn Pitt
Gloucester

SIR – Vladimir Putin has been too modest in deciding the results of his "referendums" in the occupied parts of Ukraine. 96 and 99 per cent look feeble compared to the regular 100 per cent majorities for the late Saddam Hussein and still enjoyed by North Korea's Kim Jong-un.

Francis Bown
London E3

Putting Putin in his place

SIR – The news that Russia is deploying inflatable tanks may hold the clue to another puzzle. For a while, there has been speculation that Putin uses body doubles for certain public appearances. He sometimes appears bloated or his face lacks animation. Could it be that he is also inflatable? He may even be filled with helium for a quick getaway.

William Smith
St Helens, Lancashire

SIR – Full marks to Ukraine for knocking lumps off Putin's bridge. The only slight disappointment is that he wasn't actually on it at the time.

Mick Ferrie
Mawnan Smith, Cornwall

SIR – *Putin's Bridge is falling down,*
Falling down, falling down,
Putin's Bridge is in the sea
Happy Zelenskyy

Frank Pedley
Richmond, North Yorkshire

SIR – Now that Mr Putin and the one-time food caterer Yevgeny Prigozhin are friends again, I wonder if Mr Prigozhin will bake a cake by way of an olive branch to his employer – and, if he does, whether Mr Putin will eat it.

Tom Stubbs
Surbiton, Surrey

SIR – I wonder what hotel window Prigozhin will accidentally fall out of.

Dr Trevor Masters
Southend On Sea, Essex

The French revolution

SIR – You have to hand it to the French. They may not be able to police their borders and do love a long lunch but they yield to no man when it comes to organising a riot.

Mark Calvin
Tretower, Brecknockshire

New Zealand starts anew

SIR – Jacinda Ardern has announced that she is stepping down.

I am thrilled for the people of New Zealand.

Tim Rann
Mirfield, West Yorkshire

SIR – Any chance of Joe Biden following the example of Jacinda Ardern?

Dominic Shelmerdine
London SW3

Keep watching the skies

SIR – If it turns out that these mysterious craft hovering above the US are indeed refugees from another world or just explorers, then I am not sure that blasting them out of the sky with no warning is a very sensible policy, given how advanced their civilisation must be.

After all, we in the advanced world took a very dim view of indigenous peoples who got in our way when we "discovered" them in our explorations.

Anthony Singlehurst
London SE11

SIR – You wait ages to shoot down a Chinese balloon and then three turn up at once, just like the 137 bus in Clapham.

Bernard Kerrison
Boca Grande, Florida, USA

SIR – We send £50 million annually to China; those spy balloons do not fund themselves.

Alan Sabatini
Bournemouth, Dorset

SIR – You report that China could weaponise laptops, cars and fridges for spying.

My new washing machine has WiFi; will China do the ironing or just record my collar size?

David Rumsey
Pinner, Middlesex

Playing a Trump

SIR – It saddens me (as the UK's premier Donald Trump impersonator) to read such unkind letters about the former president's minor imperfections in *The Daily Telegraph*. These can only serve to damage his otherwise flawless stature.

If such views become widespread, it could severely reduce the number of appearances I am required to make. Is this not the paramount consideration?

Guy Rose
London SW14

SIR – Now that Trump is "home", following his arrival in Aberdeen, perhaps he could stay and become Scotland's first president when it gains independence.

Peers de Trensé
London SW11

SIR – In 2016, American voters elected Donald Trump as president because he wasn't Hillary Clinton. In 2020 they elected Joe Biden because he wasn't Donald Trump. It is to be hoped that in 2024, Americans will have candidates they can vote for rather than against.

David Miller
Chigwell, Essex

SIR – Recent comments on the paucity of choice facing Americans in their upcoming presidential election do not speak of any novel situation. I recall, in 1980, asking some Americans visiting my hotel how it was that their great country was limited in choice between a peanut farmer and a B-film actor. They survived quite well, as I recall. Our prime minister thought so too.

Duncan Reeves
Lindfield, West Sussex

SIR – The secret if you are worried about falling over and not being helped up is to run for president of the United States.

Jeremy Wood
East Preston, West Sussex

Charge!

SIR – Should our forces adopt electric tanks, we'll need to ensure that any country we invade has enough charging points.

R. P. Gullett
Bledlow Ridge, Buckinghamshire

The downsides of Down Under

SIR – The job advert by BluGibbon Medical
Recruitment luring our junior doctors to Australia
with the promise of a "swim and surf in the sun" would
appear to have overlooked the sharks, snakes and
spiders. I just thought this might add a little balance.

Ronnie Cleave
Winkleigh, Devon

SIR – Britain is not the only country where you need
to watch out in case an animal steals your lunch.
In 1986 on a side trip from Adelaide to Kangaroo
Island I stopped for a snack by the beach. Leaving
my sandwiches on the roof of my car for a few
moments to retrieve a bottle opener from the boot, I
emerged to find my lunch had disappeared and – in
the distance – a kangaroo was bouncing merrily away
clutching a large paper bag.

Christopher Kirker
London SW11

All together now

SIR – In the mid-1960s I was invited to join a Scottish student group at an International Student Song and Dance Festival in Rouen. We went on a coach to a number of outlying venues to give a performance. On the way the Scottish singers warmed up with an amazing collection of obscene songs, all set to hymn tunes which other nationalities recognised. They must have left with a totally false impression of Scottish culture.

Colin Garrett
Berkhamsted, Hertfordshire

SIR – On a visit to a village bar in Normandy in the 1980s with a fellow Englishman, a song was demanded from us (in good humour) to contribute to the communal singing. The best that we could come up with was some chants we had learnt on the football terraces.

On subsequent visits to the area, I have found no evidence that "You're going home in a f—ing ambulance" caught on with the locals.

Martin Wynne
Oxford

TRAVELLING
HOPEFULLY

Hell on two wheels

SIR – Walking along a street in East London, I came across a sign as follows:

"Cyclists, slow down, pedestrians have priority".

The sign was for the pavements.

Mike Hayes
Via email

Bumps in the road

SIR – I often see vehicles marked "Highway Maintenance".

We don't want our roads maintained in their present condition – we want them repaired properly.

Andrew Blake
Marlborough, Wiltshire

SIR – With roads like these, who needs speed bumps?

Captain Peter Morgan
Tenbury Wells, Worcestershire

SIR – Seen on a Devon lane: BEWARE POTHOLES. SECURE DENTURES TIGHTEN YOUR BRA STRAP.

Donald King
Kennerleigh, Devon

SIR – During a bumpy taxi ride in the Caribbean many years ago, the driver told us he had a PHD. We were surprised to hear him explain it was for being a PotHole Dodger. Now I qualify for the same title.

Ruth Cliff
Uckfield, East Sussex

SIR – In this country we have long been accustomed to driving on the left side of the road.

Today, however, we drive on what is left of the road.

Eden Parris
Milton, Cambridgeshire

SIR – I hesitate to propose this as a solution to the tardiness of councils in filling in potholes, but a particularly egregious example in my street was dealt with – in remarkably rapid fashion – by the local authority after someone had painted a very artistic set of male genitalia around it.

Tom Stubbs
Surbiton, Surrey

SIR – Arrived here a few days ago. Roads immaculate and empty, and no potholes. Please explain.

Rosy Waddingham
Via email

On the slow train

SIR – Announcement heard at a North London railway station: "We would like to apologise for the delayed HS2 railway line. This is the result of a seriously flawed original business case."

John Stewart
Terrick, Buckinghamshire

SIR – HS2 should be renamed H2S, the chemical symbol for hydrogen sulphide, which has a distinctive smell of rotten eggs and is best avoided at all costs.

Robert Hood-Wright
Bodmin, Cornwall

Please take your seats

SIR – I see from your photograph of Sir Keir Starmer and Wes Streeting that they are both the kind of annoying train passenger who bags an aisle seat for themselves in order to keep others from sitting next to them. I hope they each paid double for their ticket to York.

William T. Nuttall
Rossendale, Lancashire

SIR – The only downside of being offered a seat on the Tube is that you have to ask yourself: do I really look old?

Judith Barnes
St Ives, Cambridgeshire

Passing the test of time

SIR – You and your readers may be surprised to hear that driving tests were first introduced in Ireland only as recently as 1964. Also, because of a postal strike in 1979, thousands of people received their full licences in that year without ever sitting a test. And, as you'll know if you've ever driven in Ireland, they're still out there. You have been warned.

William Smith
St Helens, Lancashire

SIR – I took my driving test in 1974. I was wearing platform sole shoes that were reminiscent of Elton John's boots in the Pinball Wizard video. I passed first time.

Kathleen Glennon
Whickham, Tyne and Wear

SIR – My father learnt to drive in the mid-1950s when he was in his mid-fifties. After failing the driving test six times, he wrote to the Ministry of Transport. He explained that he believed that all his examiners either suffered from peptic ulcers or had unhappy home lives. He passed his next test.

Elaine Noble
Manchester

SIR – When I took my motorcycle test in the 1960s, the standard procedure for the emergency stop part was for the examiner to leap out from behind a parked vehicle waving his clipboard. I am sure my resulting collision was not the sole example of why this methodology was later abandoned.

Peter J. Newton
Chellaston, Derbyshire

Taken for a drive

SIR – On carefully driving out of a multi-storey car park in Uxbridge I was flagged down by a policeman. I sheepishly pulled up and wound down the window and he peered at me and said: "Madam, do you usually drive with a punnet of strawberries on your roof?"

Shirley Batten-Smith
Watford, Hertfordshire

SIR – When I lived in Cyprus I related to a friend how that morning after shopping in Famagusta – a couple of miles away – I had discovered the melon I had bought sitting on the roof of my car. She complimented me on my driving. I didn't tell her my car was a soft top and the melon had nestled cosily in a dip.

Margaret Clark
Salisbury, Wiltshire

SIR – In 1967 I became the proud owner of a brand-new Ford Zephyr in aquatic jade. My pride was immediately and forever affected by my first passenger describing the experience as "like driving a large snooker table".

Ian M. Warren
Beaconsfield, Buckinghamshire

SIR – The trend towards grey and silver cars is making it increasingly difficult to play Car Snooker during a journey. It is almost impossible to pot a pink. However, we do manage to enjoy the odd game of Yellow Car.

Janet Haines
Reading, Berkshire

Heavens above

SIR – As I approach my 79th birthday I have been considering my eventual end. If I have been good, I should go to heaven. If I have been bad, I will probably spend eternity in Manchester Airport.

Rob Lawson
Sunderland, Tyne and Wear

The best thing since sliced bread

SIR – While on a short holiday recently I was reminded that there is nothing more amusing than watching the daily show which is guests battling with toasters over breakfast. It has everything from humour to jeopardy, happiness and occasional heartbreak. It's almost worth the cost of the holiday alone just for the entertainment.

Robert Stranks
Southwater, West Sussex

SIR – At a hotel in Tobermory, Mull, I asked what the difference was between the full Scottish breakfast that I had been served and a traditional full English back home, expecting to be told that the slice of black pudding had been replaced by a slice of haggis. However, the rather dour waitress replied simply: "It's in Scotland".

Bruce Denness
Niton, Isle of Wight

LONG MAY
THEY REIGN

Splitting heirs

SIR – The Duke of Sussex seems to consider his past conflicts with the Prince of Wales to be surprising and therefore newsworthy.

A better perspective might be gained by considering why, in both British Sign Language and Makaton, the sign for "brother" is two fists rubbing together.

> **David Glover**
> Colchester, Essex

SIR – The King has asked the Archbishop of Canterbury to broker a peace between Prince Harry and Prince William. Would not a more appropriate choice be Tyson Fury?

> **Anthony Haslam**
> Farnham, Surrey

SIR – I understand that Princess Diana wanted Harry to be William's wingman. Unfortunately, he has turned out to be William's whinge man.

> **Chris King**
> Woking, Surrey

SIR – Australian cricketers hold the record for the longest whinging history following their defeat in the 1932/33 "Bodyline" Ashes Series.

Harry must hold the record for the greatest whinge for the sheer size and range of his catalogue.

> **Tony Manning**
> Barton on Sea, Hampshire

SIR – I read that the Sussexes, having "stepped back" from the more arduous royal life that was expected of them, have now had enough of being in the spotlight and "after a difficult few weeks" are taking yet another "step back".

Perhaps a few more "steps back" and they will disappear from public view altogether.

Huw Wynne-Griffith
London W8

SIR – Are the Sussexes sitting at home thinking "that went rather well" or "crikey, what have we done?"

Ann Griffin
Tarporley, Cheshire

Recollections may vary

SIR – I was interested to learn from Prince Harry's ghostwriter that "the line between memory and fact is blurry".

I hope that this will be acceptable as an appropriate explanation in any future discussions I may have with HMRC.

Nick Pope
Woodcote, Oxfordshire

SIR – Crossword clue – "spare", surplus to requirement; unneeded; inessential. Harry titled his book well.

Felicity Thomson
Symington, Ayrshire

SIR – Is it too late to ask Prince Harry's publisher to add the word "us" to the title of his autobiography?

Mark Carr
Lower Froyle, Hampshire

SIR – A group of us have come up with a little challenge.

The first one to find a copy of *Spare* in a charity shop wins a packet of ginger nuts.

Susy Goodwin
Ware, Hertfordshire

SIR – Spare is described in the media as the fastest-selling non-fiction book ever. Non fiction? Some of us have opinions that differ.

Leonard Macauley
Staining, Lancashire

SIR – They say there is a book in all of us. Most of us are wise enough to not put pen to paper.

Gilly Ritchie
East Meon, Hampshire

Unhappy prince

SIR – This is like watching a posh Jeremy Kyle.

The only reputation Prince Harry is trashing is his own.

Pamela Birch
Lytham St Annes. Lancashire

SIR – Given the longevity that runs in his family, I wonder if Prince Harry has given any thought to what he might do in the future. Fifty or more years is a long time not to live as a gentleman.

Jane Moth
Stone, Staffordshire

SIR – Captain Mainwaring would have used two words to describe Harry.

Chas Batchelor
Helensburgh, Dunbartonshire

If truth be told

SIR – Nick Timothy might well be right when he suggests that Prince Harry may never have read philosophers such as Derrida but the Prince might well have read *Through the Looking Glass* by Lewis Carroll:

"When I use a word," Humpty Dumpty said in rather a scornful tone, "it means just what I choose it to mean – neither more nor less."

Poor Humpty Dumpty came to a sticky end (unsticky really).

Martin Smith
Brimpsfield, Gloucestershire

SIR – What has surprised me most about the Prince Harry phone-hacking trial is the amount of information he and his associates supposedly left on their voicemails. If any investigative journalist had been unfortunate enough to be instructed to hack my phone, the arresting headline would have been "ANGUS STILL HASN'T PHONED HIS MUM BACK".

Angus Fraser
East Dorking, Surrey

Family drama

SIR – Dig up the Bard of Avon: we have never needed him more. We should have a play, an opera, a ballet and a version of Harry on Ice, as well as the long-running soap opera.

James Omer
Banbury, Oxfordshire

SIR – Any time now I'm expecting Will and Kate to perform on *Strictly Come Dancing*.

Hugh Bebb
Sunbury on Thames, Middlesex

Carolus Rex

SIR – Some six years ago my wife and I planted a Prince Charles clematis. Our other clematis flourished but Prince Charles put on a very disappointing display and virtually disappeared during an extended period of heat and drought.

However, in September last year it sprang to life, has grown some 42 inches, is covered in buds and looks fresh and lively.

Is there a message here?

Michael Stranks
Margaretting, Essex

SIR – King Charles III may be about to get off to a very good start in challenging Queen Elizabeth II's record of 15 serving Prime Ministers during a monarch's reign.

Edward Hill
Chandlers Ford, Hampshire

SIR – My aunt, aged 91, is a retired primary school teacher. On discussing the new king, she admitted that he "shows promise". Faint praise indeed.

I can see this on his school report.

We eagerly anticipate his next one.

Catherine Damsell
Hartford, Cheshire

SIR – My three-year-old Cavalier King Charles Spaniel goes by the name Cromwell.

His Majesty should fear not as I am a Royalist.

Neil Godson
Maidenhead, Berkshire

SIR – After seeing the King's new cypher on a Yeoman Warder, I noticed a post box with E II R. For King Charles perhaps this could become C III Post Office, or C3PO.

Rob Dorrell
Bath, Somerset

The head that wears the crown

SIR – I do hope His Majesty the King will visit Geo Trumper's barber's shop in Curzon Street before his Coronation. If he wears Royal Navy uniform then a regulation short back and sides will be required.

John Pritchard
Ingatestone, Essex

SIR – I readily accept that I will almost inevitably be charged with treason, but may I humbly beseech His Majesty the King to forsake his appalling habit of putting his hand in a side pocket. The only witness I will call in defence at my trial will be the royal tailor.

Paul Fulton
Dereham, Norfolk

SIR – It would be a shame if Christ's Hospital were not able to carry the cloth of gold canopy at the King's Coronation because of "concerns that it may prove too heavy for school children". Have you seen the size of the children? My grandson who attends the school is just sixteen but can bench press 104 kg and he is not the largest in his year! Perhaps his size 12 shoes might get in the way though.

David Cross
East Preston, West Sussex

SIR – Overheard in WHSmith in Croydon, from a not particularly older gentleman: "Ah, the Coronation, they come round so quickly."

Mary Moore
Croydon, Surrey

Bring your own banquet

SIR – I am concerned that the new King may not have fully thought through the effects of his edict that peers attending the forthcoming Coronation must not wear their Coronation robes and coronets. I am told that, at the last Coronation, peers found their coronets a useful storage place for the sandwiches needed to sustain them in the long wait beforehand.

William Long
Newton Abbot, Devon

SIR – I am shocked that Jacob Rees-Mogg has cast aspersions upon Coronation Quiche because it has broad beans in it. Surely his redoubtable nanny should have sorted out any fussiness about food when he was growing up?

Fiona Wild
Cheltenham, Gloucestershire

SIR – I can assure anyone I know that they will not be offered "slimy pie" at any festivities I will be holding to celebrate the Coronation.

Shirley Batten-Smith
Watford, Hertfordshire

SIR – The problem with the French is that they have no word for "quiche".

David Chamberlain
Houghton on the Hill, Leicestershire

By invitation only

SIR -The Foreign Office has the perfect opportunity to demonstrate British diplomacy with the expectation of Han Zheng's arrival at the Coronation ceremony. Welcome him warmly and seat him at the very back, preferably behind a pillar. The Chinese will get the message.

Sonia Kleyman
Alicante, Spain

SIR – Could it be arranged that 007 is seated next to Han Zheng at the Coronation?

Angus Jacobsen
Montrose, Angus

SIR – If Harry and Meghan do decide to attend the Coronation they should be prepared for a Paddington Bear stare (or two).

Jacqueline Tomlinson
Ascot, Berkshire

SIR – The TV cameras focused on all the right people at the Coronation.

Perhaps Prince Archie could be persuaded to have a birthday every day of the year.

Ben Howkins
Staverton, Northamptonshire

Long live the King

SIR – Here endeth the longest apprenticeship in history. Long life, Sire.

Rose Woolhouse
Moreton in Marsh, Gloucestershire

SIR – Having watched the Coronation last weekend it seems clear to me that the monarch must have the following qualities: a strong character, a strong understanding, a strong determination, a strong level of patience and a strong bladder.

Brian Stanton
Sutton, Surrey

SIR – Royal crowns should be fitted with chin straps.

Ian Kerr
Coventry, Warwickshire

SIR – *Staggering* is a word I would use to describe the Coronation weekend's events.

Coronated is a word I hope never to hear again.

Tessa Worthington
Tunbridge Wells, Kent

SIR – The planning by the military for the Coronation Procession was detailed and thorough; its execution was flawless. Everything worked as it should, in sharp contrast to anything for which the Government is responsible. Time for a military coup?

Steve Davis
Abergavenny, Monmouthshire

SIR – The "Not our King" protesters in Scotland were also protesting against the cost of the Coronation. Two in 70 years sounds like careful financial management and thrift to me.

Roger Foord
Chorleywood, Hertfordshire

Penny for your thoughts

SIR – You write that "only a miracle can turn Tory fortunes around". I witnessed one at the Coronation service. She was holding a sword.

Andy Trask
Liphook, Hampshire

SIR – Over some 36 years, my long-suffering wife has had to put up with the other women in my life. First it was the Lady of Iron, Margaret; now it is the lady of the sword, Penny.

Martin Powell
Wysall, Nottinghamshire

SIR – Given the universal approval of the Lord President of the Council's performance at the Coronation, perhaps the Tories need a new pressure group. I suggest it's called: PM4PM.

Colin Cummings
Yelvertoft, Northamptonshire

SIR – Without detracting from Penny Mordaunt's important role in the Coronation, an excellent set of biceps, coupled with exemplary composure and stamina, are hardly essential qualifications for high office.

Stephen Howey
Woodford Green, Essex

Palace outsider

SIR – The end of Section 21 no-fault evictions is being proposed in the Renters (Reform) Bill.

Does Prince Andrew have friends in government?

Jonathan Mann
Gunnislake, Cornwall

SIR – Associates of Ghislaine Maxwell claim that the bath-tub depicted on the front page of *The Daily Telegraph* is too small for the sexual activity alleged by Virginia Guiffre.

I can very happily recall several encounters in a similarly sized receptacle, and would be delighted to try some more with a like-minded person – if I could escape my wife for long enough…

Tim Bradbury
Northwich, Cheshire

Fit for a queen

SIR – You report that a "soup and shakes" diet can be an effective weight loss regime. A similar gruel was offered to Queen Victoria, who had a body mass index of over 32. She found it very palatable...eating it between meals.

Ralph King
Morpeth, Northumberland

SPORTING
CHANCES

Why, why, why?

SIR – You report that the Welsh Rugby Union has banned the singing of "Delilah" as it includes words referring to domestic violence. Presumably in due course they must also ban the singing of the French national anthem given its explicit exhortation for patriotic locals to water the fields with the impure blood of visiting soldiers.

> **Dr Martin Shutkever**
> Pontefract, West Yorkshire

SIR – I'm really looking forward to watching the Welsh RU stopping the 73,000-strong crowd from singing "Delilah" on Saturday.

> **Jonnie Bradshaw**
> Wallingford, Oxfordshire

SIR – The song the Welsh Rugby Union must ban is the one that goes to the stirring melody of "Cwm Rhondda". This outrageously encourages obesity: Feed me till I want no more...

> **Jeremy Collis**
> London SW19

Kicking off

SIR – Eddie Jones says that he will not speak to the Rugby Union ever again.

Lucky Rugby Union!

Adrian Lloyd-Edwards
Dartmouth, Devon

Case of the blues

SIR – If the Oxford crew had not been wearing such silly sunglasses on a dull day, could they have won the Boat Race?

Roger W. Payne
Chelford, Cheshire

Back in the game

SIR – It was a little disturbing to see Sir Andy Murray expressing his delight at his latest victory in quite such an aggressive fashion. Given his successful surgery, surely the most appropriate response would be a gentle Hip, Hip, Hooray.

Nicholas Young
London W13

SIR – Any support for Roger Federer being the next James Bond, should he wish to pursue an acting career?

Colin Slater
Via email

SIR – Maybe Novak Djokovic could assist the Wimbledon schedulers by not bouncing the ball 16 times before each and every serve.

Ann Walker
Rotherham, South Yorkshire

SIR – Having watched Wimbledon tennis, I draw two conclusions: 1. Losing a match weakens one's bladder.
2. Spanish shorts manufacturers need to use bigger cutting patterns.

Keith Phair
Felixstowe, Suffolk

SIR – I was amused to read that a rubber duck nicknamed John QuackEnroe forms part of the All England Club's rain detection system at Wimbledon. Does it quack "You cannot be cirrus" when a cumulonimbus cloud approaches?

Jolyon Cox
Witney, Oxfordshire

The acid Test

SIR – Whenever two of the triumvirate of Australians – Mark Taylor, Ricky Ponting and Mel Jones – are commentating on the Test, I feel as if I've been trapped in a small room full of budgerigars. It seems that more words spill from their lips in a single commentary stint than the great Richie Benaud would utter in an entire series.

Michael Stanford
London SE23

SIR – Enjoying T20 cricket this evening, I noticed Phil Salt was playing for Lancashire.

Aware of Phil Mustard, affectionately known as Colonel, I wondered if there was a cricketer to make up the cruet and came upon a Michael Pepper who plays for Essex. Two of the three are wicket keepers and the third has sometimes kept wicket. Seasoned hands perhaps.

Jasmin Harries
Tavistock, Devon

SIR – I'm pretty sure the English cricket team has been the most diverse team in world cricket for decades; they even let Yorkshiremen play sometimes. Well done cricket.

Paul Gaynor
Windermere, Cumbria

SIR – To avoid confusion between the Men's Ashes and the Women's Ashes we could rename them the Mashes and the Washes.

Tony Palframan
Disley, Cheshire

SIR – I am old enough to suggest confidently that the women's version of the Ashes should be called "Cinders".

Richard Coles (age 74)
Malvern, Worcestershire

SIR – Rather than spending more money in the Supreme Court trying to remove migrants, would it not be more effective to employ Johnny Bairstow?

James Calder
Alresford, Hampshire

SIR – On a rather disappointing day for England the highlight for me was Bairstow's magnificent catch of a Just Stop Oil protester at the start of play.

Tony Manning
Barton on Sea, Hampshire

SIR – To Baz or not to Baz, that is the question. Whether 'tis nobler to Baz and lose, or to bore and win. Think I know the Aussies' answer.

Michael Hollands
Pattingham, Wolverhampton

SIR – "Bazball has died. The body will be cremated and the ashes taken to Australia."

Michael Keene
Winchester, Hampshire

SIR – So-called sledging in Ashes Tests has a long history. In the 1932/33 "Bodyline" tour in Australia it is reputed Douglas Jardine, the England captain, went to the Australian dressing room to complain at being called a b——–d during his innings. The Australian captain, Bill Woodfull, turned to his teammates and asked "Which of you b——–ds called this b——–d a b——–d?

David Saunders
Sidmouth, Devon

Man of the match

SIR – I have offered my services to the BBC to present *Match of the Day* this Saturday. Although I have not played football since appearing for my school under-11 side in the 1970s, it seems I might be the most qualified person available given all the former footballers refusing to appear on the programme.

Mark Shaw
Heathfield, East Sussex

SIR – If the BBC is looking to replace Gary Lineker and his mates, I can recommend any number of middle-aged blokes of my acquaintance, who for many years have been quite sure they could be doing a better job.

John G. Smith
London N11

SIR – On a cold, blustery, dark afternoon our local ice cream van just passed blaring out the *Match of the Day* theme tune. While I admire his sales optimism I can't help but wonder if he was making some sort of political statement.

Matthew Banks
Surbiton, Surrey

SIR – The more I hear about former footballers the more I like racehorses.

Guy Bargery
Edinburgh

SIR – Thank God for the row about Gary Lineker; at least it has got Matt Hancock off the front pages.

L. J. Remblance
Apperley. Gloucestershire

They think it's all over...

SIR – Thankfully the football season is nearly over. If I had a pound every time a commentator had used the word "brilliant" I would have been able to purchase a free season ticket and also a pie for every game.

Henry Maj
Armitage, Staffordshire

Come to the table

SIR – Some educationalists assert that a regime of outdoor sports will produce the young adults that Britain needs.

The sport of snooker is ideal for developing the personality. It requires precision in striking the cue ball, and tactics and cunning in deciding the next move. It attains high drama when there is a closely fought match, and gives the sheer joy of winning as opposed to the empty virtue of sportsmanship. It is conducted at a civilised pace, with time to draw on a cigarette while one's opponent is at the table. It sure beats the hell out of shivering in the wind and rain on a gloomy winter afternoon while a ball is kicked or thrown about on the far side of the pitch.

Michael Gorman
Guildford, Surrey

Evenly matched?

SIR – In the past we did try mixed football. One lad on my side got so frustrated with his efforts to rescue the ball from his female opponent that he physically picked her up and without breaking sweat ran up the field with her in his arms and the ball at his feet, to huge applause from all sides.

The idea of mixed football was shelved.

William Morant
Bedford

SIR – I would dearly love to be a world-class athlete, but I am short, ill-proportioned and entirely lacking in athletic ability. These are my misfortunes of birth.

There are no classes at the Olympics for those who share my physique. I could however take advantage of the general fear of age discrimination and enter for my son's school sports day. Competing against toddlers I would probably win, but I doubt it would bring me the satisfaction or acclaim that I crave.

Hetta Graham
Burgh St Peter, Norfolk

In a league of their own

SIR – If the BBC Choir wants to prevent their demise
they should don football shirts when they sing. The
BBC is besotted with anything to do with football.

Paul White
Marshfield, Wiltshire

Déjà vu all over again

SIR – Today, February 2, is Groundhog Day in the US.
May I congratulate the planners on Sky television
who, on channel 308, have scheduled the film
Groundhog Day followed by the film *Groundhog Day*
followed by the film *Groundhog Day* throughout the
whole day.

John Frankel
Newbury, Berkshire

SIR – It would seem that any resemblance between
the new BBC dramatisation of *Great Expectations* and the
original novel is entirely accidental.

Patrick Miller
Hartlepool, Co Durham

SIR – I see no harm in the latest adaptation of
Great Expectations. It is "not like the book" because
it is a clever parody. And we see a side of Uncle
Pumblechook we never expected!

Derek McMillan
Durrington, West Sussex

Happy ending

SIR – I recommend a new game to your readers –
name the lead characters who will die in the final
episode of *Happy Valley* on Sunday evening (somewhere
between 0 and 10 possible).

Well done to the BBC for not releasing the box
set. This game has kept us entertained for hours and
I have an Awards Ceremony video call booked with
friends for 10pm on Sunday.

Robert Swift
London SW15

SIR – Perhaps now that the BBC's *Happy Valley* has
finished we can now be spared the endless images of
Sarah Lancashire stuffed inside a high-vis jacket every
time we open a newspaper, magazine or switch on the
TV.

After weeks of such exposure I am surprised it's not
become the latest "must have" fashion accessory.

Michael Smith
King's Lynn, Norfolk

SIR – I haven't watched the last instalment of *Happy
Valley* yet.

I feel like I am in an episode of *The Likely Lads* when
Terry and Bob are trying to avoid hearing the result of
a football match.

It's not been easy.

G. W. Doggrell
Kingsley, Hampshire

That's not what I heard

SIR – We read that puns rate highest in enjoyable jokes. More amusing to me are the unrehearsed gaffes which occur in TV subtitles. Some examples come to mind:

– a rowing eight getting close to the bowels of the leader

– a boxer who has never eaten his rival
– GPs are seeing more peasants
– lots of near Mrs in tennis
– the Queen was most ungrateful.

Vernon Phillips
Mere, Wiltshire

SIR – According to the subtitles on my TV, the forecast for parts of the UK today is for falling reindeer. Makes you wonder what Father Christmas is doing now the Christmas rush is over.

Penny Colman
Melksham, Wiltshire

Cut to the song

SIR – I can't help but reflect that with the Coronation last weekend and Eurovision this weekend, we have, in the space of seven days, gone from the sublime to the ridiculous.

Although I accept that for many, that should be the other way around.

Robert Readman
Bournemouth, Dorset

SIR – How to win a song contest:

Rule 1 The presence of any hint of a tune is prohibited.

Rule 2 A set rhythm is not allowed.

Rule 3 Lyrics must be incomprehensible nonsense.

Rule 4 Outfits need to be either outrageously ridiculous or barely visible.

Victory thus guaranteed.

P.S. Be nice to your neighbouring countries.

D. Thom
Woolsery, Devon

SIR – It was subtle of the BBC to show Thomas Hardy's *Far From The Madding Crowd* alongside the Eurovision final. We enjoyed the Hardy.

Tony Greenham
Sutton, Macclesfield

SIR – With every group having a festival these days I see a gap in the market for a white, stale, male and female festival. We will listen to *The Archers* and drink lashings of wine, while complaining of the state of our great nation. We will need plenty of Portaloos but minimal police presence. A closing time of 8pm will ensure we are all back in our beds before the witching hour.

All we need is a snappy title so that we can market it to our target audience.

Mike Sutcliffe
Dalkeith, Midlothian

SIR – Glastonbury: where young people actually listen to old people.

Martin Brenig-Jones
Stowmarket, Suffolk

This Morning's headlines

SIR – I wonder if, for his television interview with Amol Rajan, Phillip Schofield had used the same PR adviser that Prince Andrew did for his interview with Emily Maitlis. The magnitude of "car crash TV" was remarkably similar.

Simon Oakley
Far Forest, Worcestershire

SIR – The hounding of Phillip Schofield has clearly been wildly out of proportion to his faults. For my part, I can forgive him everything except the spelling of his name, which has condemned me to years of corrections.

Philip Wedmore
London SE24

SIR – In view of the sex scandal engulfing the BBC, I am reminded of an old friend who gave me some valuable advice many years ago. "On life's long road," he said, "I have found the penis to be a most unreliable compass."

Jeremy Nicholas
Great Bardfield, Essex

SIR – The breaking news is that trust in the BBC is broken and it needs breaking up.

Chris Penney
Wellington, Somerset

Welcome to Planet Earth

SIR – Surely David Attenborough is the most appropriate point of contact for alien life.

They have much in common – both having travelled millions of miles.

Geoff Johnson
Gateshead, Surrey

A new Challenge

SIR – I enjoyed the return of *University Challenge* and it was so good to see the BBC heavily into recycling, with the new studio clearly a remnant of an old *Doctor Who* or *Blakes 7* set.

Nicholas Grenfell-Marten
Llanfaethlu, Anglesey

SIR – I was interested to see Amol Rajan's debut performance on *University Challenge*, but as soon as he said "haitch" I bounced off the wall and switched over.

Mary Harris
Sheffield, South Yorkshire

This great stage of fools

SIR – I see that in the opinion of actress Jessica Barden, "posh actors" should not play characters from poorer backgrounds.

Following this logic, only mad kings should be allowed to play *King Lear*.

Jean Moore
Kidderminster, Worcestershire

SIR – I was horrified recently to learn that the lead actors in *The Gold* had never personally robbed a bank in their lives. And Hugh Bonneville had never been a DCI.

Cynthia Harrold-Eagles
Northwood, Middlesex

SIR – Andrew Lloyd Webber was told that he could not create a musical about a certain country because he was not from there. Imagine how short the *Planets Suite* could have been. Just a lonely Earth. Holst would have rattled that off in five minutes.

Robert Ward
Loughborough, Leicestershire

Know your audience

SIR – I attended the very enjoyable live cinema screening from the Royal Opera House of Verdi's *Il trovatore* but was somewhat surprised to read in the programme notes under the heading "'Guidance":

"Suitable for ages 8+

This production contains themes of war, murder, suicide and reference to infant death."

Presumably if an eight-year-old can sit still for three hours he can cope with anything.

C. R. P. Hennis
Doncaster

SIR – I remember attending the Theatre Royal in Newcastle when a disturbance in the audience caused the performance to be halted and the lights put on. It transpired that a gentleman returning late to his seat realised he needed to raise the zip on his trousers and on doing so he had caught in the zip the hair of a lady sitting in front of him.

Sir Neville Trotter
Newcastle upon Tyne

The name's Bond

SIR – I for one would never accept 007 being female. Unless, of course, she looks, talks and walks exactly like Sean Connery.

Stefan Badham
Portsmouth, Hampshire

USE AND ABUSE
OF LANGUAGE

The long and the short of it

SIR – The Health Secretary Steve Barclay proposes a Delivery Plan for Recovering Urgent and Emergency Services. Clearly, an acronym is needed for this laudable venture. May I suggest PRUNES? This should ensure delivery.

Alan Honeyman
Scarborough, North Yorkshire

SIR – The Met's decision to adopt a "less aggressive" name for its Operation Viper anti-gun violence team is strange enough, but odder still is the change to the Proactive Armed Team. The villains must already be calling them the PrATs.

Paul Douglas
Edenbridge, Kent

SIR – The adjective smart is an acronym: System for Modifying Adult Rational Thought. Apply it to any device, phone, meter, fridge, motorway, etc. to realise how appropriate it is.

David Pynn
Malmesbury, Wiltshire

When I use a word...

SIR – I always thought the Minister for Levelling Up was responsible for the filling of potholes in our nation's roads.

William Dean
Woodbridge, Suffolk

SIR – Does anyone know what the career structure is for a Legally Qualified Chair?

Does one start as a Legally Qualified Stool, perch on a LQ Bench and eventually retire as a LQ Sofa?

Arnold Burston
Burton-on-Trent, Staffordshire

SIR – Since the police are now describing paedophiles as "minor-attracted people", which makes them seem almost normal, I suggest that a new term for criminals should be "legally averse individuals".

Andrew H. N. Gray
Edinburgh

Talking shop

SIR – I bought this morning, from our local supermarket, something labelled "indoor rhubarb". I assume this is what, before the days of woke, was called "forced rhubarb", which would now need a warning attached to it.

Patsie Goulding
Reigate, Surrey

SIR – Such a shame that the old romantic and definitive names – satsuma, mandarin, clementine, tangerine etc. – have been substituted for the prosaic "easy peelers". Peeling is not even always easy.

Jenny Funge-Smith
East Hagbourne, Oxfordshire

SIR – My dogs are happy in the knowledge that their food is gently steamed in an environmentally friendly oven for extra flavour.

Alexandra Elletson
Marlborough, Wiltshire

SIR – Placing an order with Amazon today for Royal Canin dog biscuits for an 18-month-old cocker spaniel, I was intrigued by the following:
Warning: Not suitable for children under 3 years. For use under adult supervision.

Jean Clark
Eastbourne, East Sussex

SIR – When I collected my medication from the chemist, there was a message on the label: "Keep out of reach and sight of children".
Does this mean I may no longer visit my grandchildren?

Peter Turvey
Guildford, Surrey

SIR – My new kettle came with descaling instructions that began: "Stand in an empty sink". Obviously I didn't.

Liz Machacek
Penn Bottom, Buckinghamshire

SIR – When my wife and I had a tearoom, our menu stated that "All sandwiches are served with a crisp salad". A customer one day called me over and asked where his crisps were.

Steve Cartridge
Bolton, Lancashire

SIR – I recently noticed that the deodorant I currently use is "anti irritation". I have to admit that is me to a T. My husband uses the same brand. His is "invisible". That is most definitely the effect it has on him as I can never find him when I need him to do something for me.

Stella Currie
Bramhall, Cheshire

Break the news

SIR – The next time I break something in the kitchen, I shall follow the example of Elon Musk and tell my wife that it suffered a rapid unscheduled disassembly.

Tony Hill
Stratford upon Avon, Warwickshire

Change of address

SIR – The Historic Environment Scotland might not have gone far enough in its insistence on the use of inclusive language by Scots tour guides. After all, tourists may bring along their pet dogs, and based on ever-increasing sensitivities it may soon be unacceptable to exclude them. I suggest that the least offensive way to address "mums", "dads", "sons", "daughters", "brothers", "sisters" and "dogs" is the broadly inclusive term "mammals". That should cover all tourists for the foreseeable future, and it may be millennia before excluding plants is deemed offensive.

Christopher S. Holmes
Clitheroe, Lancashire

SIR – My wife and I are decreeing that in future we are to be addressed as "Oi You".

This title has many advantages: it is gender neutral, singular or plural, and free of white privilege.

Peers M. S. Carter
Southfleet, Kent

SIR – Should there be a more gender-fluid title than "Knight Bachelor"?

Alternatively, the Prince of Wales could take the opportunity to wear a dress to present it to Grayson Perry.

Susan A. Smith
Ashburnham, East Sussex

Privates language

SIR – We are told that the word vagina is distressing to some people, so vaginas should be called "bonus holes" instead. Does this mean, in the name of gender equality, that penises must be called bonus points? I can see some scope for confusion in that.

David Cockerham
Bearsted, Kent

SIR – I have been very happy with my vagina for the last 70 years and have no desire to see it re-branded as a "bonus hole" as suggested by Jo's Cervical Cancer Trust. Apart from sounding disgusting and being anatomically incorrect I am very confused as to who receives the bonus.

Dr Catherine Keech
Guildford, Surrey

Don't judge a book

SIR – If publishers are to start to change the language of children's literary classics, as they have with Roald Dahl, due to "outdated views", wait until they hear about the works of the Grimm Brothers.

Andrew Holgate
Wilmslow, Cheshire

SIR – I'm surprised that sensitivity editors changed "chamber maid" in Roald Dahl's *The Witches* to "cleaner". My cleaner would object; she insists that she is a domestic engineer.

Peter Ledger
Ipswich, Suffolk

SIR – At the weekend, in my effort to complete *The Daily Telegraph* general knowledge crossword, I was thumbing through a dictionary and was horrified at some of the words that I came across. Should we be allowing a book like that in our schools where children and other vulnerable people might be adversely affected?

Graeme Robertson
York

SIR – As a regular lesson reader at my Church I was recently required to read a passage from Maccabees. It concerned torture, cutting out of tongues and chopping off of hands. Had it been read on any news programme it would have included a warning beforehand and a helpline number at the end.

Thankfully none of the congregation seemed traumatised, although the gin and tonics before lunch were pretty strong.

Joyce Hall
Newton-le-Willows, Lancashire

SIR – Instead of changing the word fat to enormous as in Roald Dahl's books, publishers could look to Alexander McCall Smith who has a lovely expression for Mma Ramotswe in *The No.1 Ladies Detective Agency*. She is described as being "traditionally built", a rather appealing phrase.

Carolyn Lovell
Cranbrook, Kent

SIR – I sincerely hope charity shops and book fair organisers will benefit from the influx of Roald Dahl books, donated by woke households, by adding a sticker on the front of each book declaring: "Original unedited copy".

Nigel Sergent
Horndon-on-the-Hill, Essex

SIR – To ensure this letter is suitable for a modern audience I have nothing else to say.

Edward Church
Selling, Kent

SIR – Soon words deemed offensive will be replaced by asterisks. Reading a novel will be a cross between *Blankety Blank* on television and *I'm Sorry I Haven't A Clue* on Radio 4.

Bernard Powell
Southport, Lancashire

Uncertain terms

SIR – The London School of Economics is going to now refer to the Christmas holidays as "the winter break". Apparently, the LSE authorities believe that the new name better reflects "the international nature" of their community and their "broader global engagement". Let's hope they don't have any students from countries in the Southern Hemisphere.

Gilbert Dunlop
Great Offley, Hertfordshire

SIR – You report that the word "field" has been declared by the University of Southern California to have racist connotations and will, henceforth, no longer be used.

A phrase such as "field of study" will now be outlawed and replaced with the word "practicum".

I have just written to all my email contacts advising them of my new surname.

Richard Longpracticum
Weston Patrick, Hampshire

Worrying development

SIR – I have recently become aware of a possible new pandemic which everyone should be careful to avoid.

The name of the disease is "Worries". I quite often go into a pub, for example, and when I order a drink I am told by a member of staff: "No Worries!" This I assume means that the establishment is free of Worries and I can drink in safety and comfort. This situation can be found in many walks of life and the public should be careful not to make any transactions unless they are assured that there are "No Worries".

Tim Sugg
Hope, Derbyshire

That way madness lies

SIR – The Duchess of Sussex would have the word "crazy" banned because of its negative connotations. But there are positive connotations in countries such as Greece, where being called crazy is a compliment. It means you are creative, fun, imaginative.

I speak as one who's been crazy most of my life!

Andrea Bates
Enstone, Oxfordshire

SIR – The sad news of an attack near Neuschwanstein Castle in Bavaria produced yet again the explanation that this wonderful building was created by "mad" King Ludwig II of Bavaria.

I always feel sorry for poor old Ludwig. As soon as his name is mentioned, there is sniggering and he is described as "the mad king".

But when you compare him with some of the others – Christian VII of Sweden, for example, or even Kaiser Wilhelm II – it is clear he belongs under the heading "mildly eccentric".

All right – he built extravagant castles and listened to Wagner's music – but don't we all?

Anthony C. Payne
St Bees, Cumbria

I hope you're not sitting down

SIR – "I am old and vulnerable. Please do not sit on me", is displayed in large print on antique chairs and benches at Hardwick Hall. A carefully placed teasel would be more attractive and do the job equally well.

Rosemary Morton Jack
Oddington, Gloucestershire

Nothing to report

SIR – Richard Nixon invented the "non-denial denial". In stating "I plan on running – but we are not prepared to announce it yet", has Joe Biden invented the "non-announcement announcement"?

Mike Thomas
Brill, Buckinghamshire

SIR – I note that the Met Office is now referring to "organised showers" in its forecasts.

Exactly who is organising them? If this is a new Government department, then I'm not sure they will happen at all.

Tony Cross
Sevenoaks, Kent

I'm sorry, I'll read that again

SIR – I'm grateful to *The Daily Telegraph* for regularly introducing me to words I've never seen before.

Today's is "normcore".

Dr P. E. Pears
Coleshill, Warwickshire

SIR – Reading that Mankads could be banned in club cricket I was shocked that they had any role in cricket at all. However on further reading I understood that I was confusing them with mankinis. I was much relieved.

Paul Earl
Helsinki, Finland

SIR – Until today I had assumed being demisexual meant only being able to achieve sexual satisfaction with the aid of a certain size champagne bottle.

I thank your correspondent for the clarification.

John Hutton
Worksop, Nottinghamshire

SIR – I read Bryony Gordon's Features article on Gwyneth Paltrow's wellness routine with interest. It includes something called dry brushing.

In model-making circles, "dry brushing" is a technique used to apply subtle coatings of dust, rust and general grime to a model to achieve an effect of weathering and neglect.

I think Ms Paltrow should be made aware of the results of using this technique before she does herself lasting harm.

P. Rowe
Broseley, Shropshire

Twitter ye not

SIR – Twitter's problem with the word "woodcocks" is nothing compared with the travails of my friend at a major British bank who emailed a colleague to comment on the success of his local football team, Scunthorpe United.

Bernard Kerrison
Boca Grande, Florida, United States

SIR – When I asked my Amazon Alexa device to add "fat balls" to my shopping list, my request was met with stony silence.

Happily I was able to add them manually from the app so my little feathered friends did not go hungry.

David Barnett
Newark

SIR – I was brought up on a farm, and until last week I always thought AI meant artificial insemination.

Janet Wheatley
Cardiff

SIR – Actors playing small parts in films are not described as film stars.

So why is it that those appearing in pornographic films are always described as porn stars, no matter how small their parts might be (to coin a phrase)?

Nicholas Young
London W13

The name game

SIR – A colleague and I were completing our hotel registration. Our details were being entered into a computer by the hotel receptionist.

Asked for her initials, my colleague replied "L. C.". The receptionist, exasperated after what had clearly been a long day, retorted: "So that'll be E then."

Colin Soden
Northampton

SIR – A few years ago I was asked for my full name by an assistant in a large department store, to facilitate a delivery. I said: "Lynda, with a 'Y'" and "Hughes with an 'H'". My parcel duly arrived: Linday Hugesh.

Lynda Hughes
Via email

SIR – I was lunching in a South African restaurant when the waiter overheard my friend say: "My surname is White. My parents shouldn't really have called me Aisla". The waiter said: "You should worry? My name is de Kock". I remarked that it is a common and famous name of Dutch extraction – indeed, a de Kock has recently captained the South African cricket team. "Yis," he said, "but my parents shouldn't really have called me Everard, should they?"

Alan Pearce
Verwood, Dorset

SIR – We here in Yorkshire are upset at the continued use of a Welsh name for one of our Three Peaks, that of Pen-y-ghent. A good friend of mine believes we Yorkshiremen should insist that it now be called by its Yorkshire translation, "t'big 'ill".

David Black
Osmotherley, North Yorkshire

The writing's on the wall

SIR – I once read a message carved into an ecclesiastical building which read "I hate graffiti".

Underneath some wag had added "I hate all Italian food".

Christina Pyemont
Eastbourne, East Sussex

No changes, full stop

SIR – Could someone please explain to me the definitions of "step change" and "sea change" and how they differ from a good old-fashioned change?

Sue Milne
Crick, Northamptonshire

SIR – Why must all money now be "hard-earned"?

Andy Vale
Upminster, Essex

SIR – It started with the Covid pandemic, followed by the cost of living crisis, then the threat of nuclear war, and to cap it all, the ban on the Oxford comma.

We shall survive.

John Catchpole
Beverley, East Yorkshire

SIR – I shouldn't have worried. Wimbledon can still put the apostrophes where required: "Ladies' Singles" and "Gentlemen's Singles". Perhaps things aren't so bad after all.

Liz Wheeldon
Seaton, Devon

DEAR
DAILY TELEGRAPH

Matt blackout

SIR – Could our MPs please introduce a law to punish the presenters of the *Today* programme for describing that day's Matt cartoon during the newspaper review before I have had a chance to buy my paper?

A term of five years without parole should be enough for a first offence.

Geoff Smith
Gretna, Dumfriesshire

SIR – Sanity: Matt is back!

Robert Roberts
Wrexham, Denbighshire

Fill in the blanks

SIR – I used to pride myself on my ability to finish your paper's "Toughie" cryptic crossword in an hour or so. However, last Friday's offering had me chewing on countless pencils and pulling my hair out. To no avail.

It seemed to have been compiled by a sadistic mastermind. Even with the answers revealed, some clues still seem impenetrable.

May I suggest that a classification of the level of difficulty be printed alongside – perhaps with a health warning.

Dennis Rolfe
London NW3

SIR – Is the compiler of the quick crossword going through a difficult time? Today's answers include "Siren Song", "Lothario", "Adulterer", "Split Up" and "Divorcee". It doesn't sound good.

Jan Bardey
Kineton, Warwickshire

SIR – Although I understand why in your articles it is necessary to replace some letters of swear words with dashes, sometimes it would be helpful if there were more letters included.

I spent quite a few minutes trying to complete the phrases "s----- peasants" and "B-s----y movie", and I am still not convinced I got it right.

Angela Stone
Burgess Hill, West Sussex

Photo opportunity

SIR – The wildlife of the United Kingdom is wonderfully diverse but, from the superb pictures that regularly feature on the pages of *The Daily Telegraph*, one might be forgiven for thinking that it consists entirely of kingfishers, deer and the occasional beaver.

Charles Smith-Jones
Landrake, Cornwall

SIR – The picture on the front of your features section – "Where have all the doctors gone?" – has an unintended and wry poignancy for a bygone era. Half the modern NHS medical workforce is female and no hospital clinician has been allowed to wear a tie and white coat at work for 15 years.

Dr Michael Clements MD FRCP
Chipperfield, Hertfordshire

Hold the front page

SIR – The headline on your front page ran: "Sting exposed British embassy guard as spy".

Why are the security services depending on fading pop stars to do their work? Have the cuts really got that deep?

Brian Gedalla
London N3

SIR – Is the juxtaposition of the article "Sex makes you live longer" with "Why I can't wait to be 80" a positive editorial decision or just a fortuitous fluke?

Kate Trelford
London W5

SIR – Apparently it is Blue Monday today, and there is yet another breakfast smoothie recipe in Features. At least it is not green. Ah, but wait. At bedtime, a milky chamomile tea concoction is recommended. Neither will "boost my happiness hormones".

Linda Hepburn
Chatham, Kent

SIR – I was momentarily taken aback by the byline on your Letters web page which, inter alia, lists "Ashes whingeing". I would like to make it known that Mrs Ashe and I never indulge in whingeing. Well, hardly ever.

Philip J. Ashe
Leeds, West Yorkshire

We regret to announce

SIR – As a regular reader of the Announcements in the *Telegraph*, I am concerned that the once regular offering of "Thanks to St Jude for prayers answered" has ceased.

Is the state of the country now so dire that even the Patron Saint of Hopeless Causes has given up?

Tony Bevington
Bristol

SIR – An analysis of death notices published in *The Daily Telegraph* during the month of January 2023 shows that in the 349 notices where the age was given, the mean age at death was 87 years and 6 months. In the same period the mean age in the 261 notices published in the *Eastern Daily Press* was lower, at 84 years and 5 months.

As the difference is statistically significant I have instructed my children to publish my death notice in *The Daily Telegraph* – but they have suggested I might be less of a drain on the NHS if I opt for the *Eastern Daily Press*.

David Ray
Norwich

Great minds think alike

SIR – I've just read David Frost's article and am delighted to know that in addition to the six chaps I will meet in the pub tonight there is one other person in the country with an understanding of how real life works, or doesn't.

Geoffrey Sharples
Newport, Shropshire

SIR – I suggest that the new political party to replace the Tories at the next election should be the *Telegraph* Letter Writers' Party. All problems solved.

Owen Hay
Colchester, Essex

SIR – Your instructions for sending letters to the editor state:

"We accept letters by post, fax and email only."

I'm curious to know which other methods have been attempted over the years and the circumstances that necessitated curtailment.

Nicholas Hart
Surbiton, Surrey

SIR – Enjoyable though it is, letter-writing is time consuming. When I told a friend recently that I was contemplating cutting back, he threatened to cancel his subscription to the newspaper.

I therefore feel duty-bound to continue.

Nicholas Young
London W13

SIR – I notice that senders of letters to the *Telegraph* from retired armed service personnel are followed by their former rank. Could this be extended to us lesser mortals?

Ink Monitor Bernard Wilson (retd)
Ramsbottom, Lancashire

SIR – Does my appearance in Here *We Go Again…*: *Unpublished Letters to* The Daily Telegraph, ironically, make me a published author?

Roger Willatt
Lyndhurst, Hampshire

SIR – Disgusted of Tunbridge Wells has been replaced by Frustrated of Ingatestone.

John Pritchard
Ingatestone, Essex

SIR – I long to be offended. Unfortunately, as my wife pointed out, I'm a middle-aged, middle-class, heterosexual, non-religious white male so I'm not allowed to be.

George Adams
Brading, Isle of Wight

SIR – Winter is coming, and I shall shortly go into hibernation mode, as promised, with an occasional break for a stroll, stretch and scratch.

No use asking me then for solutions to problems that have already been given many times over.

Liam Power
Dundalk, Co Louth, Ireland